BECOMING THE HERO
OF YOUR OWN LIFE

BECOMING THE HERO OF YOUR OWN LIFE

THE LIES THAT BIND *and the* PROBLEM WITH HAPPILY EVER AFTER

M. A. SHANESY, PsyD

BECOMING THE HERO OF YOUR OWN LIFE © copyright 2022 by Mary Auster Shanesy. All rights reserved. No part of this book may be reproduced in any form whatsoever, by photography or xerography or by any other means, by broadcast or transmission, by translation into any kind of language, nor by recording electronically or otherwise, without permission in writing from the author, except by a reviewer, who may quote brief passages in critical articles or reviews.

ISBN 13: 978-1-63489-454-8

Library of Congress Catalog Number has been applied for.
Printed in the United States of America
First Printing: 2022
26 25 24 23 22   5 4 3 2 1

Cover design by Zoe Norvell.
Interior design by Patrick Maloney.

Wise Ink Creative Publishing
807 Broadway St. NE, Suite 46
Minneapolis, MN 55413

wiseink.com

To Kelsey, Nick, Dan, and Cadence, who always believed in the Hero in me—even when I didn't.

CONTENTS

Introduction   1

Chapter I
Good Mental Health and the Great Lies
11

Chapter II
The Problem with Happily Ever After
21

Chapter III
I Can't
35

Chapter IV
Never, Always, Perfect
43

Chapter V
No Choice
49

Chapter VI
The Personal Lies
57

Chapter VII
The Hero's Journey
67

Chapter VIII
The Magic in a Pill
73

Chapter IX
The Stages of Change
83

Chapter X
The Objective Observer
93

Chapter XI
Identifying the Lies
101

Chapter XII
Examining the Evidence and Challenging the Lies
111

Chapter XIII
Overcoming the Obstacles:
Anxiety, Depression, and Trauma
127

Chapter XIV
Committing to Becoming and Being a Hero
145

Chapter XV
Why You May Want to Find a Therapist
151

Chapter XVI
If You Are a Therapist
165

Chapter XVII
Reward, Return, Resurrection:
Living as the Hero of Your Own Life
169

Exhibits
The Great Lies   177
The Personal Lies   179
Facts versus Opinions   183
Challenging the Lies / Examining the Evidence Worksheet   185
Techniques for Coping with Anxiety and Depression   187
Using Humor to Cope with Stress and Challenges   197
For a Better Night's Sleep   201

Acknowledgments   203
About the Author   205

INTRODUCTION

*The truth may be out there, but the
lies are inside your head.*
— **TERRY PRATCHETT**

If someone told you a lie—something you knew to be untrue, inaccurate, a misrepresentation—would you believe it?

Would you build your world around that lie? Would you build yourself around it? Would you embrace it as truth and share it with people you love, respect, and trust, giving it a life beyond your own?

"Of course not!" most of us say with a sense of affronted dignity. We pride ourselves on knowing what is true and what isn't. Truth is important because that sense of truth and lies gives us a feeling of security and comfort as well as a sense of control over ourselves and our world. We need that sense of security, comfort, and control in a world that's often uncomfortable, disappointing, frightening, dangerous, and chaotic.

But what if you're wrong? What if the things you've known—the things you've been told are true, the things you've held as true throughout your life and the lives of those you love, respect, and trust—are untrue, inaccurate, a misrepresentation?

What if our world, our lives, and our selves are built on

a complete and complex fabric of lies so familiar and pervasive that we never even think to question them? What if those lies have been a part of our earliest memories as well as the earliest memories of our parents, our grandparents, and everyone who has been an important part of our lives and the world in which we live?

Would you believe those lies even though they create the myriad forms of distress that afflict so many of us? Would you believe the lies that are the source of so much depression, sadness, anguish, anxiety, worry, stress, and substance abuse?

Of course not.

And if you had the real, unwavering ability to see the truth and turn away from the lies, you would most certainly look at everything through the eyes of truth and free yourself and those you love from not just the lies, but also depression, sadness, anguish, anxiety, worry, and stress.

We all would. And we all can.

We can learn to see the truth from the lies. We can learn to free ourselves from the slavery and suffering that lies impose on us. We can learn to live the lives that only the truth can make possible.

We can live as the Heroes of our own lives.

This book was written for everyone who wants to learn to separate the truth from the lies and change their life. It was written for people who are tired and worn down by sadness and who never feel quite good enough. For anyone who is exhausted by constantly trying to think around every corner so they can be safe, knowing they will never succeed. For people who have tried everything they can think of and feel defeated by the knowledge that they are missing something. For people who want to be the Hero of their own life.

This book was also written for therapists who have given everything they know and have learned and still struggle to see their own truth. For therapists who try to help, want to help, and still feel helpless in the places where their clients get caught. For therapists who want to become the Heroes of their own lives and want to help the people they work with become Heroes as well.

This book was written out of my personal and professional Hero's Journey.

Like most of us, I was raised by good parents who tried to give their children the best life they could. And, like most of us, they raised me with the lies, Great and Personal, that led me to distress I didn't understand and couldn't seem to get free from.

By my twenties, I had completed the first phase of my education and had entered the adult world. I was independent, on my own. I had a good job, a nice apartment, and good friends. I was smart, well liked, and successful. But I was also unhappy, lonely, worried, and confused. I had done everything I was told were the "right things to do" by my parents, my family, my friends, my teachers and mentors, and the world in which I lived. And still I was unhappy, lonely, worried, and confused. I couldn't figure out what I was missing, what I was doing wrong.

I was also lucky. I was lucky because around that same time, a friend shared with me that she was in therapy because she was unhappy, lonely, worried, and confused. Without knowing I was doing it, I took my first step on the Hero's Journey and found a therapist. I remember telling that therapist that I'd had "a normal, happy childhood.

I'm smart, successful. I have a good life. So why do I feel this way?"

I was lucky because I found a therapist who helped me learn to examine my thinking and the beliefs, assumptions, biases, prejudices—the lies, Great and Personal, although she didn't call them lies—that were enslaving me and keeping me stuck in misery. She helped me learn to become an Objective Observer, separating FACT from OPINION. She helped me learn to challenge the lies, Great and Personal. She guided me on my Hero's Journey to find my path and become the Hero of my own life.

I was lucky because, around this same time, I discovered a couple of brilliant thinkers and writers. The first was Alice Miller, a Swiss psychoanalyst, who wrote a book I often recommend to people I work with. *The Drama of the Gifted Child* opened my eyes to the impacts of my "normal, happy childhood" experiences on the adult I had become as well as the lies, Great and Personal, that were enslaving and torturing me, keeping me stuck in misery.

The second was Joseph Campbell, who wrote *The Power of Myth* and was recognized in his lifetime as one of the leading authorities on the myriad ways in which cultural and personal myths have informed and shaped human lives and experience through the ages. This book is where I first encountered the Hero's Journey and the possibility of becoming the Hero of my own life; and it profoundly changed the way in which I understood my world, my life, and my choices.

Then, in my forties, a watershed in my professional life led me back to school, this time to pursue a doctorate in clinical psychology. In the course of my studies, I learned the many theories surrounding the lies, Great

INTRODUCTION

and Personal, and the many different schools of thought surrounding what to do about them; and I began working with individuals to help them relieve their own suffering.

My professional experiences have involved working with people of all ages and from all walks of life. Female and male, old and young, business people and homemakers, incarcerated offenders and "normal," average people trying their best to get through their days with a sense of contentment and purpose. People who are suffering with depression, anxiety, trauma, substance abuse, loss, and grief. People who are unhappy, lonely, worried, confused, lost, just as I was so many years ago. People who are yearning to understand and to free themselves. People who desperately want to become the Heroes of their own lives and don't know how.

As I worked with these individuals, the lies, Great and Personal, appeared again and again as the source of their suffering. The more I worked with people who were experiencing distress they didn't understand and couldn't free themselves from, the more I became aware that embarking on the Hero's Journey was the critical step we all must take. We all must take this critical step because the Hero's Journey can give everyone the knowledge, awareness, and vision that can set us free to become the Heroes of our own lives.

I have lived the freedom and power of the Hero's Journey in my own life; and over the course of my career, I've been privileged to help, guide, and mentor many on their own Hero's Journey. I have witnessed the power of selfhood, and by becoming the Hero of your own life, you too can end the distress and suffering that living the lies, Great and Personal, can create. I have watched people face, wrestle with, and challenge these lies, Great and Personal, to find their own truth and create the lives they have dreamed of so they are no longer stuck, no longer enslaved to misery.

This book was written as a roadmap of the Hero's Journey to freedom and selfhood. It begins at the beginning, of course, with an exploration of what good mental health looks like for all of us. Thousands of pages have been written about mental illness, but little to nothing about good mental health, which is the destination we're all aiming for. But if you don't know where you're going, any road will take you there. So a definition of good mental health, our ultimate destination on the Hero's Journey, is where we'll begin in chapter I.

From the definition of good mental health, I'll identify and describe the four Great Lies—those universal "truths" we've all heard that are part of our earliest memories as well as the earliest memories of our parents, grandparents, and everyone who has been an important part of our lives and the world in which we live. In chapters II through V, you'll learn the details of the Great Lies and how to recognize them in your thoughts and feelings. You'll learn about the problems with Happily Ever After, I Can't, the absolutes that make up NAP (Never, Always, Perfect), and No Choice, and how they get us stuck and enslaved by the distress they create.

After the Great Lies, we'll identify, explore, and explain the Personal Lies in chapter VI. These are the lies that come to us most directly from our personal "authorities": our parents and caregivers, our elders and teachers. The Personal Lies are a reflection of our personal histories as well as the personal histories of our personal

INTRODUCTION

"authorities." They are the biased perspectives, the biased "truths," that are passed on to us before we're old enough to venture into the world to find our own truths.

Understanding what the lies, Great and Personal, are, and developing the ability to recognize them is all about awareness and knowing what we're dealing with. Awareness is a critical step; however, unfortunately it's not enough to free us from the slavery of lies and release us from misery. We must take the Hero's Journey, challenge the lies, and learn the truth in order to become the Heroes of our own lives. There are many ways to do this, but they all begin with the Hero's Journey. The common elements and stages of the Hero's Journey will be mapped out in chapter VII.

Since the Hero's Journey begins with the refusal of the call, and finding a sage or mentor in order to cross the threshold from the known to the unknown, it seems reasonable to ask, "Can I do it on my own? Do I need help? And if so, what kind of help?" There are many potential answers to these excellent questions, but chapter VIII will explore the lie that our culture, science, and industry would have us believe: that there is magic in a pill. Examination of this lie will involve reviewing what has been learned from fifty years of science and research into the relative effectiveness—and ineffectiveness—of antidepressant and anti-anxiety medications as well as what years of helping others has taught me.

If medication isn't the answer—or not the only answer—how do we answer the call to begin the Hero's Journey? When it comes to facing and challenging the lies, Great and Personal, that have enslaved and created so much misery for so many of us, the willingness and ability to answer the call is related to a social science theory known as the stages of change. The five steps in these stages are detailed in chapter IX to enable each of us to identify our readiness to answer the call and embark on the Hero's Journey. From precontemplation, to contemplation, to preparation, to action, and finally maintenance, these stages help us understand the change process we must undertake in order to become the Heroes of our own lives.

Earlier I mentioned that there are many ways to challenge the lies and learn the truth. Once we decide to answer the call, one of our first steps in challenging the lies is to develop the ability to be an Objective Observer. Being an Objective Observer means taking in or dealing with facts and/or conditions without distortion by personal feelings, prejudices, assumptions, or interpretations. In chapter X, you'll learn how to separate fact from opinion and become an Objective Observer by simply looking at, hearing, or perceiving someone or something as it most simply and obviously exists.

Once you've answered the call and become an Objective Observer, it's time to work on identifying the lies, Great and Personal, that have kept you stuck, enslaved, and miserable. So in chapter XI, you'll learn to recognize the link between something happening in the world around you and the uncomfortable feeling that's the result of the automatic negative thoughts created by the lies to which you fall victim. You'll also understand the value and critical importance of writing down the automatic negative thoughts and lies so you can take the next step on the Hero's Journey to challenge and vanquish them.

Now that you know how to recognize and identify the automatic negative thoughts and lies, you can begin to

INTRODUCTION

examine the evidence and challenge the lies. This is where your newly acquired skills as an Objective Observer will be your secret weapon, because the lies have been in your head so long that they may seem like truth to you, disguising themselves as things "everybody knows." This is also where you'll learn to allow yourself to explore *all* the possibilities, not just the ones that come into your head or that you've always known. I'll lead you through some examples in chapter XII so you can begin to see how examining the evidence and challenging the lies is not only possible, but also the key to breaking the chains that have enslaved you and kept you stuck in misery.

Chapter XIII will get even more specific with challenging the lies that keep many of us stuck in anxiety, depression, and the effects of trauma. I'll again use examples of the lies, Great and Personal, that most often create anxiety, depression, and the effects of trauma, as well as the kinds of challenges that have led to the rewards of freedom, selfhood, and the life of the Hero for me, and for the individuals with whom I've worked over many years.

Having answered the call, faced and overcome the tests and challenges, and triumphed in the ordeal, I'll walk with you on the path of reward, return, and resurrection as the Hero of your own life. Because even though reward, return, and resurrection may have changed us, they likely haven't changed our family, friends, bosses, colleagues, or the world around us. So how do we hang on to the truth of our reward? How do we hold tight to our selfhood and continue to walk the path of the Hero when the lies, Great and Personal, are still controlling and enslaving those around us? Chapter XIV will complete the roadmap of the Hero's Journey and create an understanding of and compassion for the possibility that we may need to make the roadmap a permanent fixture in our lives.

Chapters XV and XVI will circle back to consider whether you may want to find a therapist to help you on your Hero's Journey and, if you are a therapist, how you may want to consider using these concepts in your own Hero's Journey as well as your work helping others on their Hero's Journey. Our loved ones, friends, and colleagues are often eager to listen and help us talk through what may be troubling us. However, these sections will explore the difficulty inherent in hearing and believing those closest to us as well as the value of a trained, objective professional.

Having completed your journey, the final chapter XVII will take you on a trip into the life you've always imagined and always wanted, a life that is finally within your grasp. I'll help you build the vision of how you can live as the Hero of your own life now and in the future, no matter what that future holds. You'll hear more of my own story as well as the stories of others who have completed their own Hero's Journey, and are living in their own truth, their own selfhood, as the Heroes of their own lives.

So, having come full circle, where do we start?

Why, at the beginning, of course.

CHAPTER I

GOOD MENTAL HEALTH AND THE GREAT LIES

We're going to have to let truth scream louder to our souls than the lies that have infected us.

— B. MOORE

In the beginning, we need a definition of what success and a healthy outlook that are free from lies look like. We need a definition of good mental health. The problem is that the people charged with creating that definition have never come up with one.

The art and science of diagnosing and treating mental health concerns appears to be as old as humanity itself. Archaeologists have discovered prehistoric human skulls with large holes cut into them through trepanation, a practice believed to cure a range of ailments including mental health difficulties. The first description of symptoms that medical historians believe to have been of mental illness associated with senile dementia is ascribed to Prince Ptah-hotep of Egypt in 3000 BC. The oldest known classification system of mental illness dates to 1400 BC, in which mental illnesses were grouped by seven kinds of demonical possession. Since that time, virtually every culture and civilization have developed methods for describing human mental and emotional problems.

Hippocrates is generally credited with being the first physician to reject supernatural or divine explanations for illness and is recognized for introducing psychiatric problems into the domain of medicine. He proposed that disease was a product of environmental factors, diet, and living habits, and that the appropriate treatment for a mental disorder depended on which bodily fluid, or *humor*, had caused the problem by being out of balance with other bodily humors.

Many scholars and researchers have observed that cultural beliefs and values play a large part in the development of what is called *illness* versus what is called *health*, and that this cultural or values bias is often invisible to individuals who share the culture. For example, compare the contemporary Western classification of animals (e.g., mammals, insects, birds) to those of the ancient Chinese (e.g., embalmed, owned by the emperor, trained, sucklings, sirens and mermaids, fabulous, abandoned). This comparison brings up two important points: first, that the same or similar phenomena can be categorized in strikingly different ways across cultures and times; and second, that all classification systems, however seemingly objective, are developed and agreed upon by humans to meet particular human needs.

The human need to classify and organize thoughts, feelings, and emotions is driven largely by the desire to identify and understand an underlying "reality" to these experiences. It also reveals what the culture defines as *mental illness* versus *mental health* as well as appropriate treatments to restore people to good mental health. In contemporary American culture, the American Psychiatric Association (APA) and the American Psychological Association have been arguing for decades—yes, decades!—over a definition of good mental health that they can all agree on. And as a result, they have come up with nothing.

The latest publication by the APA, which is the *Diagnostic and Statistical Manual of Mental Disorders*, Fifth Edition (DSM-5), devotes 947 pages to detailed and explicit definitions of what constitutes mental illness and how to recognize the symptoms that characterize it. Throughout much of recorded history, diagnosticians have generally considered the relationship between symptoms and their provoking cause or context as an essential part of understanding and identifying mental disorders. The first such effort was published in 1917 by the APA; and like every volume of the DSM that followed, it was heavily influenced by the work of Emil Kraepelin, who argued that a classical medical disease model should be applied that examined symptoms, course, and prognosis to define distinct physical pathologies.

This medical disease model was strongly championed and advanced by Robert Spitzer, who chaired the development of DSM-III and was an outspoken advocate for conceptualizing mental disorders as a subset of medical disorders. In essence, the publication of DSM-III in 1980, with its biomedical model, "medicalized" mental illness by defining it in medical terms, described it using medical language, and treated it with medical interventions.

However, even at that time, this medical disease model was brought into question, most notably by Thomas Szasz in his equally heralded and reviled *The Myth of Mental Illness*. Szasz argued that to be a true disease, the entity must first be capable of being approached and measured or tested in some fashion. Second, to be confirmed as a disease, a condition must demonstrate pathology at the cellular or molecular level. Finally, a genuine disease must also be found on the autopsy table, not merely in the living individual, and must meet pathological definition rather than being voted into existence by the APA. Szasz concluded that while individuals may behave and think in ways that are very disturbing and that may resemble a disease process, this doesn't mean they actually have a disease. Instead, Szasz characterized most of what was then and is now described as mental illness as "problems in living."

According to a journalist writing about Szasz in 2006, when speaking with one of his students, Szasz asked:

> What exactly are you treating? Is feeling miserable—and needing someone to talk things over with—a form of medical illness? Has she got an illness called depression, or has she got a lot of problems and troubles which make her unhappy? . . . Does the psychiatric term depression say more than the simple descriptive phrase unhappy human being? Does it do anything other than turn a "person" with problems into a "patient" with a sickness?

Thus, the APA and the DSM turn us into patients with a medical illness, rather than people with problems in living, and focus on what is "wrong" with an individual. The only significant response to this focus on what is "wrong" with an individual came in 1998, when Martin Seligman, then the president of the American Psychological Association, helped develop the theory of positive psychology, which is defined by the Positive Psychology website as "the scientific study of what makes life most worth living" or "the scientific study of positive human functioning and flourishing on multiple levels that include the biological, personal, relational, institutional, cultural, and global dimensions of life."

Proponents of positive psychology urge a focus on what is "right" with individuals. Practitioners of this theory are just as concerned with strengths as with weaknesses, as interested in building the best things in life as in repairing the worst, and as concerned with making the lives of normal people fulfilling as with healing pathology. Positive psychology doesn't say or imply that the very real problems people experience should be ignored or dismissed. Rather, it advocates that what is good in life is as genuine as what is bad, that what is good in life isn't simply the absence of what is problematic, and that the good life requires its own explanation, not simply a theory of disorder stood sideways or flipped on its head.

Thus, modern psychology is caught between what is "wrong" and what is "right," or what is "black" and what is "white." That isn't very helpful in a world that most of us experience in a wide and changing variety of "grays" and still not a usable definition of good mental health. How are we to know where we're going or when we've arrived without knowing the destination?

So I developed my own definition. After all, when working with individuals to help them solve their "problems in living," I always start with a treatment plan: a definition of their particular problem and a general roadmap for how they will get to a healthier place. A treatment plan is actually an individualized definition of good mental health. Helping people develop an achievable treatment plan made me realize that in order to become the Hero of our own lives, we all need a broad definition of what that would mean—of what good mental health looks like, feels like, and lives like. So, out of my experience of becoming the Hero of my own life and helping others over many years as a therapist, I developed the following.

I believe good mental health is the ability to feel everything from deep sadness (even despair) to real happiness (including great transcendent joy) and everything in between, without getting stuck anywhere. Good mental health means the ability to experience and tolerate the feelings we like and the feelings we don't like. It means we have to learn to look at and live with things we don't like and don't have the power to change or control.

It's easy to look at, revel in, and bask in the feelings we like, even when the feelings we like aren't good for us. We experience that feeling whenever we eat that entire carton of ice cream as a "reward" or to "feel better" after something goes wrong or when we're unhappy: it's good while we're in it, and terrible afterward. We also experience that feeling whenever we blame ourselves for things entirely out of our control. That way, if we feel like if it's our fault, then we're in control of what to do next time. It's not so easy to look at feelings that make us uncomfortable, unhappy, frightened, anxious, or distressed. But unless we learn to look at and live with the feelings we don't like, we can become slaves to them, stuck and terrorized by what we imagine they can do to us. We create a monster in the closet.

You may have heard of the monster in the closet—or even had one living in a closet of your own. Oftentimes when young children are sleeping in their own room for the first time and their parent has turned off the lights, wished them a good night, and pulled their door mostly closed, a little voice will call out, "There's a monster in the closet." Most parents will rush back in, turn on the lights, and comfort the child by looking in the closet, under the bed, and in the toy chest to reassure them that they are safe. Having looked, the child is usually able to go to sleep, secure in the knowledge that there is nothing that can creep out and hurt them when they close their eyes.

But what happens if that little voice calls out and no one comes to help them? What happens if the only person the child has to turn to tells them to just "go to sleep" and invalidates the child's feelings and fears without proof? Well, without the knowledge that there is nothing bigger, stronger, and more horrible that can creep out and hurt us when we close our eyes, the monster gets bigger, stronger, and more horrible the longer we don't look. And as the monster becomes stronger, it holds us stuck in the terror of what we imagine the monster might do.

When we create a monster in the closet, we give it supernatural powers and strength. We create a supervillain, just like the ones we see in movies, television, and video games—one we believe will overpower, overwhelm, and even destroy us. We believe that facing or challenging that supervillain, that monster in the closet, is an impossible task. This may happen when we hear ourselves saying things like:

- "I can't talk to strangers. I never know what to say, and I'll feel stupid."

- "I can't tell my daughter I can't give her any more money. She'll be mad. She won't love me anymore, and I'll be all alone."

- "I can't tell my boss that I can't work overtime. She'll make me feel bad."

- "I can't tell my husband he drinks too much. I'm afraid of him when he drinks."

- "I can't say no. If I do, then they won't like me anymore."

Those thoughts and fears—those lies, Great and Personal—are the ways in which the monster in the closet, the supervillain, grows bigger, badder, and stronger. They convince us that we're weak and helpless, and that we have no choice but to give in and accept the misery. We don't like those thoughts or feelings; and since no one has ever told us that we have the power to face down the monster in the closet and vanquish the supervillain, we cower under the covers and just try to hang on and get through it. We choose not to turn on the lights. We choose not to look in the closet. Instead, we turn away from those feelings, thereby giving them horrible power over us.

But there is another way.

We don't have to live in fear, anxiety, hurt, and disappointment. To find another way, we must learn to look at and live with the feelings we like and the feelings we don't like without creating a monster in the closet, without getting stuck, and without becoming slaves to one feeling or another. We must feel and experience everything from our past, our present, and our imagined future, and then learn to weave it all into a meaningful and satisfying tapestry of our lives.

When I talk with individuals about trusting themselves to feel everything and learn about their own deep ability to "handle" life, they often seem to get a little panicked. They may say things like, "I can't do that! I don't know how to do that! I don't want to do that! Is there a pill I can take? A surgery I can have? A way to deal with the monster once and for all, and make it go away forever?"

We've all felt this way at some time or another because we live in an instant gratification culture. We've all heard this description. We're constantly bombarded by our computers, smartphones, social media accounts, and televisions with stories and promises about getting rich quick, staying young forever, losing twenty pounds in a week without dieting, having a great body without exercise, looking perfect, being perfect, raising perfect children—all of it instantly and without any effort. Even science has tried for decades to sell us on the idea that there are easy, quick answers to every problem we face. These stories and promises are compelling because we want to believe them. We want to believe that there is "magic" out there that can make our lives into that dream we've carried inside forever. The problem, though, is that by looking for answers outside of ourselves, we've lost the ability to believe in our own power to know ourselves, focus on our goal, and attain it without the intervention of the latest wonder drug, fad diet, plastic surgery, or lottery ticket.

Good mental health—the ability to feel and tolerate everything without getting stuck; the ability to learn, solve, and manage the challenges and problems that can plague all of us—is something we can come to know, focus on, and achieve without a drug, diet, or any other one-time offer. We can achieve a healthy outlook and good mental health, and have the ability to feel and tolerate everything without getting stuck, by freeing ourselves from the slavery of lies.

We get stuck when a lie sneaks in—and lies are really, really good at sneaking in and making us slaves to misery, sadness, anxiety, envy, and a host of other things that make us suffer. Lies are good at torturing us because we're often not even aware that the thoughts in our heads are, in fact, lies. Because lies come in all shapes and sizes and are so common in our lives and our culture, we often don't even see or recognize them for the lies that they are. The lies that bind are there from our beginning—and even before our own beginning—and in order to free ourselves from this self-imposed slavery, we have to be willing to feel and live with everything.

"Wait a minute!" you may be saying. "Everything? We have to learn to feel and live with good and bad, fear and joy, hurt and triumph, pain and pleasure, worry and laughter, tears and agony and ecstasy? All of it? *Everything?*"

Isn't good mental health feeling good all the time? Aren't we supposed to be happy and on top of things? Isn't that what we're all striving for? To be happy? Isn't that the end of every good story, every movie, every fairy tale we ever heard or were told? Aren't we all supposed to be trying for "and they lived happily ever after"?

Actually, no.

Although Happily Ever After seems to be the moral and cultural value that we've accepted and embraced, that moral and cultural value—that end we all reach for—is the source of so much distress . . . because Happily Ever After is the first of the Great Lies.

CHAPTER II

THE PROBLEM WITH HAPPILY EVER AFTER

Above all, don't lie to yourself. The man who lies to himself and listens to his own lies comes to a point that he cannot distinguish the truth within him, or around him, and so loses all respect for himself and for others. And having no respect, he ceases to love.
— **FYODOR DOSTOYEVSKY**

There are all kinds of lies in our lives.

There are the goofy lies we believed when we were too young to know any better that we finally figured out on our own as we grew up. Maybe you remember, "If you don't stop making that face, it will get stuck that way," or "If you swallow your gum it stays in your stomach forever," or "You have to wait an hour after eating before you go swimming, or you'll drown." We can all recognize, and even laugh at, those "absolute truths" we believed when we were too young to know any better as the lies they so obviously are. Now, with the perspective of years, we know them to be untrue and would no more follow those "absolute truths" than we would tell them to our own children and loved ones.

Then there are the well-meaning white lies we tell when we don't want to be too direct, or hurt the feelings of or get into a disagreement with people we care about. Think of how many times you've said things like, "No, the roast isn't overcooked," or, "I love the sweater you gave me," or, "Your new girlfriend is great."

And then there are the Great Lies. One of the most insidious and destructive Great Lies generally starts with the phrase "once up on a time." It's a stock phrase used to introduce a story of past events, typically in fairy and folk tales. According to the Oxford English Dictionary, it has been used in some form in storytelling in the English language since at least 1380. These stories often then end with another phrase: "and they lived happily ever after." These tales, which we first encounter as children and often go on to tell our own children and grandchildren, powerfully affect the way we think about ourselves and our relationship with the world. Without our being aware of it, fairy tales shape our thoughts and goals.

Therein lies the problem. We build our selves and our lives, dreams, goals, and plans around something that is not achievable for anyone. Not just not achievable for you because you're not good enough, smart enough, rich enough, pretty enough, big enough, or strong enough. Happily ever after isn't achievable for anyone. Ever.

Take a moment right now to think about the *happy* people you know or have known. As you reflect on their lives, do you believe these *happy* people have never struggled, lost a loved one, or been hurt, disappointed, turned down, turned away, fearful, or anxious? Of course not! Hurt, disappointment, grief, and loss are inescapable parts of being alive. And yet we've been told from our earliest memories that it's possible to live happily ever after, that it's possible to live a lie.

We build our selves and our lives, dreams, goals, and plans around a lie. And research is beginning to find that it's not even really good for us, or particularly satisfying, to be happy all the time.

And what do we mean when we say *happy*? We all speak English, so we all think we mean the same thing when we use the same words. But often we mean very different things. And *happy* is one of those words we all use, like *depressed* and *anxious*, that means different things to different people. Does *happy* mean lots of money? If you won the lottery, would you be *happy*? Even though research shows that a significant percentage of lottery winners declare bankruptcy within ten years of getting all that money? Does *happy* mean having a big house? A fancy car? Traveling the world? The envy of those around you? Does *happy* mean you're loved? Have lots of friends? A partner? Children? Success? And what would success mean to you? Would it be the same success as your family? Your friends? The world in which you live?

Being happy is such a strong and familiar concept in our modern world, but almost nothing had been done to define and study the idea until recently. In 2017, a cross-cultural study of 2,324 university students from the United States, Brazil, China, Germany, Ghana, Israel, Poland, and Singapore was conducted and found that people may be happier when they feel the emotions they desire, even if those emotions are unpleasant ones such as anger or hatred. The lead author of the study, Maya Tamir, stated:

> Happiness is more than simply feeling pleasure and avoiding pain. Happiness is about having experiences that are meaningful and valuable, including emotions that you think are the right ones to have. All emotions can be positive in some contexts and negative in others, regardless of whether they are pleasant or unpleasant.

For example, someone who feels no anger when reading about child abuse might think she should be angrier about the plight of abused children, so she wants to feel angrier than she actually does in that moment. A woman who wants to leave an abusive partner but isn't willing to do so may be happier if she loved him less.

Across cultures in this study, participants who experienced more of the emotions they desired reported greater life satisfaction and fewer depressive symptoms, regardless of whether those desired emotions were pleasant or unpleasant. Maya Tamir went on to observe:

> This study may shed some light on the unrealistic expectations that many people have about their own feelings. People want to feel good all the time in Western culture, especially in the United States. Even if they feel good most of the time, they may still think that they should feel even better, which might make them less happy overall.

The happiness frenzy in the United States is a relatively recent phenomenon. According to *Psychology Today*, fifty books on happiness were published in 2000. By 2008, that number grew to 4,000. The most popular class at Harvard University in 2009 was Positive Psychology, and at least one hundred other universities offered similar courses. Happiness workshops for the post-collegiate set abounded, and life coaches were promising bliss to prospective clients.

But all is not necessarily well. By some measures, as a nation we've grown sadder and more anxious during the same years that the happiness movement flourished. In the wake of this happiness frenzy, a number of scholars, researchers, and practitioners began to observe that our preoccupation with happiness had come at the cost of sadness, an important feeling that our culture has tried to banish. In *The Loss of Sadness: How Psychiatry Transformed Normal Sadness into Depressive Disorder*, authors Jerome Wakefield and Allan Horwitz argue that when sadness is labeled as pathological depression and the full range of emotions isn't tolerated, the feelings and emotional expression of sadness or pathological depression tend to elicit hostility and rejection. In the culture of happiness, there are mass media, social media, cultural, and personal messages that imply that any confusing or distressing feeling, including sadness, can and should be eliminated.

Not surprisingly, depression has become a central concern and feature in American culture. Americans are no longer simply sad, down, or a bit blue. Instead, they are *depressed*. It's as though, culturally and linguistically, depression has become so much a part of *normal* life that individuals shape and describe any form or level of distress as depression. People will talk with family, friends, and mental health professionals about *my depression* as though it's a closely held, cherished possession as well as a disease that must be driven away in order to restore selfhood and banish all of life's ills and difficulties.

These messages spurred Mark D. Rego to ask these questions in a 2005 article for *Philosophy, Psychology & Psychiatry*:

> What will it mean to medicate away the painful experiences common to all our lives? Will we as individuals lose the opportunity for personal growth by avoiding the need to tolerate negative and painful mental experiences? Will some special perspective be lost by reducing our access to the bleakest of human experience?

Furthermore, a recent article published in *Psychological Review* suggested that when individuals are in a negative mood state, they become more analytical, critical, and innovative, and that these qualities are crucial to creating new ways of perceiving and being. Depression and sadness are signals that something is broken in your life and that you need to bear down and mend it. In this view, the disordered and extreme thinking that accompanies depression, which can leave you feeling worthless and make you catastrophize your circumstances, is needed to punch through everyday positive illusions and help you focus on your problems.

Evolutionary psychologists have even begun to hypothesize that sadness and low to moderate levels of depression may be adaptive, since they lead the individual to withdraw and ruminate, to try to understand and make up a loss or avoid a similar loss. Emotions have evolved to help the individual survive better. Fear is an emotion that helps an individual escape from a dangerous situation, while pleasure encourages an individual to try to repeat the actions that gave rise to it. Depression or sadness may serve a similarly important function.

A study by evolutionary psychologists Paul W. Andrews and J. Anderson Thomson Jr. in 2009 indicated that the brain's ability to enter a depressed state has been preserved throughout evolution, suggesting that depression is an adaptation. This adaptive depressive state promotes focused and analytical thought that can be very productive, particularly in terms of solving complex social and interpersonal dilemmas.

When you experience a loss of someone or something you love, it's normal to feel sad. Romantic breakups are sad. Losing a big client and not getting the promotion you were hoping for is disappointing. Not getting picked for a special team may hurt your feelings. These and countless other situations may cause us to feel normal sadness. But they can also be the catalyst, the step to something better. Without that catalyst, that change to try or do something different, we're likely to keep making the same mistakes and bad choices and end up in the same place we don't like. As Albert Einstein famously observed, "Insanity is doing the same thing over and over again and expecting different results."

Now, none of this is meant to romanticize depression or support a culture of sadness. Deep, long-lasting depression, with its unrelenting hopelessness, loss of energy, lack of motivation, isolation, and lack of appropriate self-care, is a serious condition that often requires professional help. Fortunately, most individuals will never experience this depth of depression. And according to the National Institute of Mental Health, the vast majority of people who experience depression are reporting mild to moderate symptoms.

However, even mild to moderate depressive symptoms can be distressing and need to be addressed in a way that accepts a middle ground. Accepting and embracing the full range of emotions are the keys to living a meaningful life, utilizing our gifts, and living with thought and purpose. Living a life that allows for that full range of emotions helps us to confront annoyances and crises with grace. It allows us to learn, stretch, and grow, which sometimes involves discomfort. It allows us to confront negative feelings head-on without letting them overwhelm us. It allows us to face and defeat the monster in the closet and to understand that living "happily ever after" isn't possible, desirable, or even good for us.

Jane, a lovely woman in her eighties, came to see me after the death of her husband of more than fifty years. She had raised four sons and lived a full life with her husband, and now he was gone. Her husband had managed their lives in a way that allowed this woman to focus on caring for her family. When he developed a long, debilitating illness and dementia, it became impossible for him to manage their lives. Jane stepped in with strength, grace, and dignity. For more than a decade, she was the rock the family clung to and relied on.

"My sons are counting on me," she said, "and I won't let them down. They need me to be strong. I can't give in to feeling bad or letting them—or anyone—see me come apart."

When Jane's husband died, the lovely, strong, resilient woman who had managed and coped and been strong for so long found that she didn't know how to let herself feel bad. She didn't know how to allow herself to recognize and honor her own feelings and to let herself grieve. And the Great Lie that we all must be happy all the time was hurting her, enslaving her, by not allowing her to feel the completely normal and natural sadness that was not only appropriate for her situation, but also what her sons likely needed from her.

Jane and I worked together on learning to recognize the presence and destructive quality of the Great Lie that we should be happy all the time, as well as ways in which she could allow herself to feel and express her sadness without fear of it harming her or her sons. She created time and space in her life for her feelings; and by doing so, she created time and space in her life for others to help and comfort her. As a result, Jane was able to work through her sadness and grief much more quickly than she would have been able had she pushed these feelings away and created a "monster in the closet." Importantly, Jane also provided a model for her sons in terms of healthy ways to experience and express the sadness and grief as a normal, natural part of life.

What happens when we don't allow sadness? Ed, a father of a nine-year-old daughter and an eleven-year-old son, lost his wife of twelve years to cancer. In an effort to shield his children—and himself—from sadness, Ed decided that they would change their lives completely. For two years after his wife's death, Ed tried hard to make everyday life different. Family gatherings were different. Holidays were different. The school year was different. Vacations were different. Ed was not going to allow his family to suffer and face their loss and grief, and so they tried to run away from feeling bad.

When I met Ed at the end of those two years, he was struggling with his children, his work, and his family. Fearful that they couldn't handle the grief and sadness of losing a beloved wife and mother, Ed and his children were now unable to handle much of anything in their lives. Ed and I worked together to recognize, honor, and manage all the emotions he was feeling around his wife's death—grief, loss, anger, confusion, the inability to successfully be a single parent—rather than allowing him and his children to be victimized by the feelings they had unsuccessfully tried to run from.

Sadness is so normal and natural to our life on this planet. I imagine you can't find a single individual who hasn't experienced it—and yet the Great Lie tells us that we're all supposed to live "happily ever after." No wonder so many of us find ourselves thinking and feeling there must be something wrong with us when everyone else is living "happily ever after." Because when normal sadness occurs in our lives, we're totally unprepared. We have little experience with how to feel and manage this all-too-human emotion in a healthy way.

But sadness isn't the only uncomfortable emotion that can be good for us. It turns out that other distressing feelings can also be good for us, and necessary for us as well.

Take anxiety, for example. Most people will tell you that they hate feeling anxious, that anxiety paralyzes or controls them. They can't leave the house, talk to people, or take a deep breath. They can't sleep, relax, or enjoy much of anything—and they don't know how to make it stop. They just want their anxiety to go away so that they never have to feel that way again. But according to the Yerkes-Dodson law, making anxiety go away would mean that many of us would never do or achieve anything.

In 1908, psychologists Robert M. Yerkes and John Dillingham Dodson discovered that there is an important relationship between anxiety and performance. In their experiments, they discovered that rats could be motivated to complete a maze with slight electrical shocks. But when the shocks were of the higher degree, their performance level decreased and they simply ran about, seeking an escape. It was clear from their work that higher arousal/anxiety levels helped to focus attention and motivation on the task at hand, but only until an optimum point.

One of the best examples of the Yerkes-Dodson law is the anxiety most people feel before taking a test. If your anxiety level is at an optimum balance, then you'll find

THE PROBLEM WITH HAPPY EVER AFTER

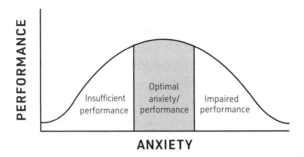

yourself performing better and remembering the right answers to the questions. However, if you're overly anxious, you'll feel so nervous that you'll be unable to remember the information you specifically learned for the test.

Another example of this law can be seen by looking at an athlete's performance. Hitting a penalty shot at the last minute of the game can be a nerve-racking moment for a soccer player. At that instance, if his desire to score is ideally balanced with arousal (anxiety), he will stay composed and score a goal. However, if he's too stressed out in the moment, he might hit the ball too slowly, hit the goalposts, or miss the goal completely.

The Yerkes-Dodson law also states that, for easy tasks, the higher the level of physiological or mental arousal—in other words, anxiety—the higher the performance. But if the task at hand is difficult, a higher level of anxiety will only increase performance to a certain point. From that point on, a higher anxiety hinders performance, because the person becomes too anxious and stressed and can't concentrate on the task. At low arousal, people are lethargic and perform badly. As arousal increases, performance also increases—but only to a certain point, after which increasing arousal actually decreases performance. Arousal in this context can also be thought of as stress or anxiety, which is felt as an inner motivating tension. The conclusion is that we usually perform better at moderate levels of anxiety.

The original research by Yerkes and Dodson was based on rats in mazes. There was one correct way through the maze, and wrong routes gave electric shocks. They were looking for the optimum punishment in which the rats would learn quickest. And as the voltage increased, learning increased as well. But beyond a certain voltage, the rats' performance decreased. They would slow down, freeze, and retreat rather than risk more nasty jolts. They even started forgetting which route was safe and which ones were dangerous. While unkind to rats, this showed how increasing stress or anxiety only motivates until the point at which the stress or anxiety, rather than the task, becomes the increasing focus of attention.

Without some motivating tension or anxiety, we have no reason to act. In this way, stress or anxiety can be thought of as a good thing. We're built to be motivated by stress.

Imagine that you're offered a huge sum of money for doing something you're perfectly good at. While normally you would perform the task well, the possible reward would weigh heavily on your mind, distracting you and increasing the likelihood that you would make a mistake.

The problem is that too much stress can cause performance to decline, sometimes sharply. A downturn can also be caused by excessive attention to a task such that extra factors that are important are missed. The behavior in the downturn is called *satisficing* and is differently motivated from the earlier stages. Rather than gaining satisfaction or reward from actions, the person who is satisficing seeks any way of reducing their stress. This usually leads to the individual using suboptimal solutions, which accounts in part for the performance decline.

But so what if a rat in a maze, somebody taking a test, or an athlete in a big game benefits from their anxiety? How does that apply to us?

Actually, we all need some degree of anxiety in order to be the best that we can be. Just as our culture and values made a devil out of the normal sadness that can help us be more creative and effective in thinking about and solving our "problems in living," our culture also decided that anxiety is another devil when, in fact, a moderate level of anxiety is vital to helping us achieve.

I've worked with hundreds of people over the years who have told me some version of this story about anxiety. Matt, for example, was a bright, capable young man who had finally found a job he really liked and wanted to do well at. He came to me, though, because he was so anxious with his coworkers that he would "say the wrong thing" at work. He described how he would go to work and feel unable to say the simplest things to the people who worked around him.

"I'm so anxious that I can't even make eye contact anymore," Matt said. "I'm sure everyone must think there's something wrong with me. I mean, who can't just come in and say hello in the morning?"

As Matt and I worked together, we were able to identify that his anxiety developed out of his desire to do well and be liked in a job he enjoyed after years of struggling to find work that engaged him. When I asked whether it was possible that Matt's anxious reaction might be alerting him to the need to pay attention to others, and the need to put some of the effort and enjoyment he found in his work into the people who work with him, Matt's face lit up. "So my anxiety is really like an early warning system to let me know that this is important to me?" he asked. "And I can do something to be prepared and succeed just like I do with a big new project?"

"Exactly," I said.

"Okay. But what's that something I can do to prepare?"

Once Matt was able to recognize that his anxiety could be seen as an ally in his desire to succeed at something that was important to him, he was able to turn his attention to problem-solving and figuring out how to take control of his anxiety rather than letting it control and enslave him. Once he stopped demonizing anxiety by looking at it as simply a reaction to something that was important to him, Matt didn't have to be a victim to it. We continued to work together for some time afterward to identify things he could do when he became aware of his anxious reactions so he could calm himself and use his abilities to work for him on his Hero's Journey.

Now I imagine you may be reading this and thinking, "But I'm anxious all the time. I worry about everything. I can't sleep, and I get overwhelmed. I can't change what's happened to me or what other people make me feel. I want to not be anxious, but I just can't. It's too hard, too much. I get too stressed out. I can't do it."

Can't is an interesting word—and another of the Great Lies.

CHAPTER III

I CAN'T

We lie the loudest when we lie to ourselves.
— **ERIC HOFFER**

We tell ourselves this lie all the time.

Can't is a handy word that makes things not doable, achievable, or possible. *Can't* lets us off the hook, means we shouldn't even try. *Can't* gives us a reason to believe that we don't have a choice, that we're not responsible, that there is no sense in going after something, even if that something is something we really, really want.

Can't is a killer of potential, wishes, hopes, and dreams. It prevents us from actually letting ourselves try to make it all come true and have the lives we want. *Can't* tells us that we have no other choice, but the truth is usually closer to *I won't* or *I don't want to*. It usually comes with the thought, "I can't do that because if I do, then . . ." *Can't* is a lie that makes us slaves to the lowest common denominator in ourselves, tells us we're less than we are, and forces us to accept being the least—rather than the best—we can be.

The best we can be is how we describe our heroes. According to the Oxford English Dictionary, a hero is "[a] person who is admired for their courage, outstanding achievements, or noble qualities; the chief character in a book, play, or film, who is typically identified with good qualities, and with whom the reader is expected to sympathize; and, the best or most important thing in a set or group."

Aren't each of us supposed to be the chief character in the book, play, or film of our own lives? Don't we all need and want to be the Hero of our own lives? The lead character that we admire, emulate, and aspire to be? That special someone who knows how to be, what to say, and what to do? That special someone who stands out from others, on their own two feet?

Heroes are often the people who do what other people tell themselves they can't. Anthony Jerome "Spud" Webb is one of those heroes. Webb, who played in the National Basketball Association (NBA), is best known for winning a Slam Dunk Contest despite being one of the shortest players in NBA history and one of only two players under six feet tall to win it. (NBA.com lists him as five feet, seven inches tall.)

Webb was born in Texas and used basketball as his inspiration. Growing up, he wasn't tall, but he used his quickness and jumping ability to outplay the bigger kids. In his first game in middle school, he scored 20 points. He could dunk the ball when he was only five feet, three inches tall. On his high school varsity team, he averaged 26 points per game. After college, most scouts predicted that Webb would end up playing in Europe or for the Harlem Globetrotters because of his height, but he was drafted in the fourth round of the 1985 NBA draft. Spud Webb played 814 games in his NBA career, registering 8,072 points, 1,742 rebounds, and 4,342 assists in twelve seasons.

Now most people would say that anybody who is five feet, seven inches tall can't play professional basketball or win the NBA Slam Dunk Contest. But Spud Webb

I CAN'T

decided he could, and he did. Webb didn't tell himself, "I can't." He wouldn't be satisfied with being less than he could be and refused to believe the lie of *can't*.

We can imagine that Webb took stock of his love of basketball and his capabilities and skills, and then gave himself permission to be everything he could be. He questioned the *fact*—which was, in fact, a lie—that anybody who is five feet, seven inches tall can't play professional basketball or win the Slam Dunk Contest. Webb critically and analytically examined the *facts*, came to the understanding that *can't* is a lie, and refused to be enslaved by that Great Lie.

And refusing to be enslaved by a Great Lie is to become a Hero, to be "the best or most important thing in a set or group." To be the Hero of your own life. To be a Hero to those around you. To be respected and admired for being the best you can be and choose to be. To throw off the chains—the lies that bind you—and succeed in having the life you've always dreamed of.

One of my favorite definitions of a Hero—and a definition we can all achieve—comes from the poem "Success" by Bessie Anderson Stanley:

> He has achieved success
> who has lived well,
> laughed often, and loved much;
>
> who has enjoyed the trust of
> pure women,
>
> the respect of intelligent men and
> the love of little children;
>
> who has filled his niche and accomplished his task;

who has left the world better than he found it
whether an improved poppy,
a perfect poem or a rescued soul;

who has never lacked appreciation of Earth's beauty
or failed to express it;

who has always looked for the best in others and
given them the best he had;

whose life was an inspiration;
whose memory a benediction.

This is the definition of someone who has rejected *I can't* and embraced *I can*, *I will*, and *I am*. An individual who has decided to become a Hero in their own life by their own choices and actions and has refused to accept a lie that encourages them to be less than who they can be and who they are.

Joseph Campbell has described the Hero's Journey in this manner:

> ... [W]e have not even to risk the adventure alone; for the heroes of all time have gone before us; the labyrinth is thoroughly known; we have only to follow the thread of the hero-path. And where we had thought to find an abomination, we shall find a god; where we had thought to slay another, we shall slay ourselves; where we had thought to travel outwards, we shall come to the center of our own existence; where we had thought to be alone, we shall be with all the world.

One of my clients, Phillip, first came to my office as (in his own words) a twenty-eight-year-old "diseased and deformed old man." He had been diagnosed with ulcerative colitis, a lifelong disorder of the digestive tract that can cause serious complications and pain, as well as a hereditary disorder of the bones in his foot. From the time Phillip was quite young, Phillip's mother, wanting to protect her son, made clear to him all the things he "couldn't ever" do if he wanted to live a reasonably long, relatively painless life. "You can't live the way other people live," she had told him. "You can't eat the foods other people eat. You can't put any stress on the joints in your legs and feet. You can't do any of this without me helping to protect you." To complicate matters even further, Phillip's father had died during Phillip's early teens, and so his mother had also told him, "You can't live your own life because I'm a widow, and I need you to take care of me."

Phillip had been caught in the prison of *can't* and had struggled with depression around this for as long as he could remember. He was an attractive, smart, funny, capable, analytical guy who had built a successful career using his good mind to think objectively and critically to find potential solutions to difficult problems. In Phillip's work world, there was no such thing as *can't*.

On the other hand, Phillip's personal life was a minefield of *can't*. "I can't exercise or lift weights, even though it makes me feel good," he told me. "I can't enjoy meals with other people. I can't tell my mother that she has to take responsibility for her own life and let me live mine. I can't tell my mother to stay out of my relationship with my wife. I can't, I can't, I can't."

Do you remember reading earlier in this chapter that *can't* is a handy word that makes things not doable, achievable, or possible? It reinforced the ideas that Phillip was unable to survive without his mother and that she was unable to survive without him despite the fact that she, too, was a successful professional. *Can't* gave Phillip a reason to believe that he didn't have a choice, and so there was no point, no hope, no sense in trying to find potential solutions to life much like he did at work. It became the killer of Phillip's potential, wishes, hopes, and dreams. It prevented him from even trying to make it all come true and have the life he wanted. *Can't* was able to do all of this because it was attached to the thought, "I can't do that because if I do, then . . ." Some of Phillip's specific *can't* statements from that time included:

- "I can't learn to manage ulcerative colitis, and so I can't eat with other people, because if I do, then I'll be in unbearable pain."

- "I can't get exercise to take care of myself, because if I do, then I'll damage and further deform my feet."

- "I can't create boundaries with my mother that keep her out of my relationship with my wife, because if I do, then she will be upset to be excluded from an important part of my life."

- "I can't ask my mother to take responsibility for herself, because if I do, then I'll be a bad person."

The phrase *I can't* tried hard to convince Phillip that misery was all he could hope for or expect. And not surprisingly, that was exactly what brought Phillip to me. But in the course of our time together, he worked hard to become the good objective observer, critical thinker, and creative problem solver in his personal life that he was in his work. When we recognized and respected that Phillip clearly had these capabilities and knew how to use them at work, he began to pose the same kind of *I wonder* statements about his life problems that he used to find solutions to his work problems:

- "I wonder how I might find some way to get control of the ulcerative colitis so I can enjoy eating with other people."
- "I wonder if there are any forms of exercise that won't hurt my feet."
- "I wonder how I might firmly, lovingly, and respectfully say no to my mother in order to say yes to my wife."
- "I wonder how I might manage and live my life, and make it clear that I'm responsible for no one other than myself."

Phillip learned how to reject *I can't* and embrace *I can* and *I will*. He decided to use his strong, positive abilities to be an objective observer, critical thinker, and creative problem solver in every aspect of his life so he could make his own choices, take his own actions, and steadfastly refuse to accept a lie that encouraged him to be less than who he can be and who he is. Toward the end of his therapy, Phillip asked, "Do you remember when I used to describe myself as diseased and deformed?" He chuckled. Phillip had become the Hero of his own life; and like many other Heroes, he did what other people tell themselves they can't.

Interestingly, people who reject *I can't* also usually refuse to be enslaved by the third of the Great Lies: NAP, or Never, Always, Perfect.

CHAPTER IV

NEVER, ALWAYS, PERFECT

*The lies we tell other people are nothing
to the lies we tell ourselves.*
— DEREK LANDY

Never, Always, Perfect. (Or NAP, for short.)

These are words we've all heard. Words we've often heard associated with rules, facts, and truths we must live by. And like all the Great Lies, these words are often the source of the expectations, feelings, thoughts, and actions that create suffering for so many people. What is it about these words that makes them so powerful and destructive? What makes them the third of the Great Lies?

Well, for one thing, these words are all absolutes, and absolutes are trouble. By definition, absolutes aren't subject to any limitation. They are unconditional, having no restriction, exception, or qualification. Absolutes carry a kind of moral authority that makes them appear to be unquestionable "ultimates." They act as a moral authority that we're taught and that we learn—a moral authority that's subject to the same cultural values that are informed and created by the personal and pervasive culture in which we're raised.

Moral authority reflects what is acceptable and unacceptable, what is good and bad, according to the cultural values at the time. This is just like the moral authority and cultural values that have decided what defines mental illness and mental health. They aren't really absolutes at all, but rather a reflection of the ideas and values that will best support the prevailing, dominant culture and what we were taught.

It sounds silly now, but there was a time when it was well known in the prevailing culture that you should never eat a "love apple," an early name for the tomato, because they were poisonous. There was also a time when, in the same prevailing culture, a woman became "unmanageable" and her uterus "hysterical," and removing it would restore her. Similarly, there was a time when people from cultures other than our own were thought of as uncivilized, unintelligent savages or heathens, and they needed to be "saved" from themselves by becoming assimilated into our own culture.

To quote Joseph Campbell again: "In a wasteland, people are fulfilling purposes that are not properly theirs but have been put upon them as inescapable laws. This is a killer." Absolutes are, by definition, "inescapable laws" that are imposed on us by others and often limit—and sometimes kill—the authentic self, or the Hero.

Also, an absolute is an ideal, a conception of something in its complete form, without fault or flaw—something that's unable to grow, change, or be improved. A definitive form that's unable to grow, change, or improve is a problem for human beings. Because human beings are organic systems, and organic systems can only exist in one of two states. Whether they are flowers or viruses, animals or people, organic systems are either growing and changing, or they're dying.

All organic systems must grow and change . . . or they die.

This means that all individuals must grow and change, or they will die—physically, mentally, and emotionally. And as discussed earlier, evolution is constantly working on organic systems—including people—to move them toward growth, change, improvement, and adaptation. So any absolutes that render individuals unable to grow, change, and improve are enslaving and killing us. Absolutes are lies that are binding us ... and killing us.

Finally, absolutes are ideals, and ideals exist only in the imagination. They aren't real or actual. Ideals like Never, Always, and Perfect are a lot like Communism—a wonderful idea that isn't achievable. Ever. By anyone at any time.

We need ideals. They are ideas that give us goals toward which to strive. Communism, when written with a little *c* (as in *communism*), is an idea where we use our own gifts and talents for the benefit of everyone, and everyone else uses their gifts and talents for our benefit. This form of communism is a wonderful ideal. But Communism with a capital *C* is what we get when individuals take the lowercase ideal of *communism* and try to make it real and actual in a very limited and specific way to meet limited and specific ends, at a specific time in history, constrained by the moral absolutes of the prevailing culture and values system.

We all know how well that turned out.

But that isn't to say that ideals aren't valuable. We need ideals because they give us direction for the ways in which we might grow, change, and adapt. Ideals become ideas that live in our thoughts and minds, which is where they belong, and are helpful to us. Ideas open us up to limitless possibilities and options to many avenues for solving problems. But when we take an ideal—something that exists only in the mind, in the imagination—and insist that we need to make that ideal real and actual, we lose sight of the limitless possibilities and options. We lose sight of the positive purpose of ideals and give our selves and our lives over to a lie that enslaves and tortures us.

When we insist that there is only one way to think about an issue or a problem and we force ourselves into only one possibility or option, we willingly give up our power of choice. When we allow ourselves to believe the lie that there is only one avenue, only one option, we give up our power. We willingly allow ourselves to be taken over, enslaved, and controlled by the lie; and when we allow this to happen, our suffering begins.

You know those thoughts. You know how they limit you, take you hostage, and extract a terrible price:

- "I can never do that."

- "I always have to do this."

- "I have to be perfect."

- And in many ways worst of all, "I can never do this *and* I must always do that because I have to be perfect."

These are often the thoughts that people who are trapped in anxiety, depression, the aftereffects of trauma, and substance abuse experience. These are the thoughts filled with the Great Lie that makes the empty promise of control, safety, comfort, acceptance, and love—the Great Lie that tells us we can finally be worthy of safety, comfort, acceptance, and love if only we do exactly as we're told and do it perfectly. These are the thoughts that people who suffer with obsessive compulsive disorder and eating disorders live with. These are thoughts that we all deal with before we find the courage to become the Hero of our own life.

These thoughts limit and narrow our limitless vision and choices to only one tiny pinpoint, to only one confined, tightly controlled, and torturous path. These absolutes limit and narrow our very selves. They bind us to lies that don't allow us to grow, change, and adapt; lies that don't allow us to live and become the fullest, best, and most fulfilled people that we can be. They bind us to lies that are killing us by turning us into people who are bound up by thoughts and feelings of worthlessness, hopelessness, and anxiety, because we're trying to solve an unsolvable puzzle: how to live with an absolute and become an ideal.

I've often worked with parents of school-age children who talk about how overwhelmed and run off their feet they feel from taking their children to soccer practice, and swim practice, and dance lessons, and gymnastics, and hockey practice, and scout meetings, and trying to be sure that homework gets done, and everyone gets fed, and gets to bed at a decent hour in order to start it all over again the next morning. When I ask why they have their children enrolled in so many activities, the most frequent response is often, "Well I have to. It's what we all have to do these days to be good parents. The kids always have to be busy with something." My most frequent question in response is, "Will the not-busy-enough police come and take you away?" The bewildered look I often get from those parents tells me that they've fallen victim to the well-known, prevailing cultural absolute that they must keep their children always busy and never idle in order to be perfect parents.

These thoughts, these absolutes, these lies, work by convincing us that we have no choice, that we *must* do what they tell us. We allow these lies to control us by accepting that we have no choice. We allow ourselves to be enslaved in a prison of *no choice* and are rendered helpless by it. We allow ourselves to be tortured by the thoughts and feelings of the absolutes and lies we've learned, and we accept that we have *no choice* but to suffer.

And, as I'm sure you've figured out by now, *no choice* is the fourth and final Great Lie.

CHAPTER V

NO CHOICE

The truth hurts, but the lies kill.
— **TERRY MARK**

In the contemporary mythic movie trilogy *The Matrix*, Neo, a Hero, seeks a truth that can save mankind and set them free from the slavery of lies created by the Matrix, the prevailing culture and moral authority of the time. In keeping with the Hero tradition, Neo sets out on a journey that takes him to the Source and to the revelation that choice is the key to freedom and selfhood. Without choice, human beings became slaves to the Matrix—a culture that enslaved them and makes them into soulless, selfless things that fuel the system that's using and killing them.

Joseph Campbell observed that the Hero tradition was a journey within, a journey for our own truth, freed from the past with "its truths, its goals, its dogmas of 'meaning,' and its gifts: to die to the world and to come to birth from within." He argued that the Hero's Journey was meant to represent a spiritual journey in an often meaningless world of trials and tribulations, to find or create a sense of Self containing substance, worth, value, and true honor; and that this is "fashioned from within."

This Self that I mentioned above is fashioned by choice. Choice is critical. It validates our sense of selfhood.

Choice states that we've acted out of our self, our knowledge, our own authentic and deeply held values, rather than out of what we've been told, what we've learned, or what has been forced on us.

When we give up choice by believing and accepting the lie that is "no choice," we give up a part of our selfhood. We sacrifice who we are, who we can be, and who we want to be. When we believe and accept *no choice*, our self loses voice and fades to nothing. When we believe and accept *no choice*, we often begin to question our substance, worth, value, and true honor.

Because *no choice* is a lie.

We always have a choice. We always have many choices.

We may tell ourselves we have *no choice* because we don't like many, most, or all of the choices we have. Or we don't like the consequences of many, most, or all of the choices we have to make. It seems easier to believe the lie and accept that we have *no choice* rather than face our choices head-on. It seems easier to not make a choice knowing the likely consequences or outcome of acting on our choices.

I imagine you may be thinking that it's easier to simply not choose. Perhaps you're even saying, "Why should I choose anything when choosing may make my life harder? I don't have to make any choices. I can stay out of it. I can simply not choose and just not deal with any of it."

Unfortunately, not choosing is also a choice. It's impossible to simply not choose, because it's impossible for human beings to remain static and uninvolved in the flow of life in and around them. It's impossible for an organic system to do anything other than choose to grow and change, or choose to die. Whether we like it or not, whether we want to or not. Whether we believe we choose, or not—we always choose.

We choose when we act, and we choose when we don't act. So if we have no choice about *no choice*, we must accept and face our choices head-on, make them with the knowledge of the likely consequences or outcomes, and act on those choices in order to achieve selfhood and live a life that reflects and honors the highest and best selves we want to be and can be.

It's unfortunate and sad how many parents with grown children have come to me with the Great Lie of *no choice* at the center of their misery. These parents love their children completely. They would—and have—done anything and everything for their children as they were growing up and beyond. These parents have been committed to being the best parents they could possibly be, and they believe they have *no choice* but to love their children unconditionally in order to be the best parents they can possibly be. These are the parents who have come to me because their twenty-, thirty-, forty-, or even fifty-year-old children are still living with them and making their own lives—and their parents' lives—miserable.

Unconditional love is another interesting and difficult concept. The difficulty with *unconditional* is that, by definition, it's an absolute; and as we talked about earlier, absolutes are trouble. Remember that absolutes have no restriction, exception, or qualification. Absolutes carry a kind of moral authority that makes them appear to be unquestionable "ultimates."

For many people, unconditional love implies that they must give or receive love, no matter what. And *no matter what* is often interpreted as having to accept, support, or endorse anything and everything that we or other people do. Unconditional love is often referred to as "mother's love," "God's love," or "true love"; but it appears to mix up and mistake two very different things. For many people, unconditional love means that you have to love and accept both the individual and all of their actions and choices without question, comment, or concern—even when those actions or choices are in conflict with your values and beliefs, or when those actions or choices put your life, or the lives of your loved ones or the person making the choice, in jeopardy.

That's where the lie slips in. It does so when we confuse a feeling such as love with how we or other people react to our actions, choices, and behavior. We may believe that if someone loves us, they will support all of our decisions and choices. Or that if we love someone, we have to support all of their decisions and choices. Or that we must sacrifice our own future, values, and beliefs—our own selfhood—to support the other, no matter what.

But if you knew that someone you loved had a drinking problem, would you take them out for a night of bar-hopping? Would you give them money to go drinking? If you knew that someone you loved had a problem with other substances, would you pay their rent, mortgage, or car payment because they had spent all of their money on those substances? Would you look the other way if they stole money from you? Would you tell yourself you had to accept, support, and enable bad decisions and unhealthy or life-threatening choices because they are your child and you love them unconditionally, no matter what? Would you tell yourself you had to accept, support, and

NO CHOICE

enable your child's bad decisions, even though those decisions harm both you and your child?

The parents who come to me believe they have *no choice* about supporting their children unconditionally, without limits or consequences, because they love them unconditionally. These are the parents who will say things such as the following:

- "I have no choice about my thirty-five-year-old son living in our basement. He has nowhere else to go. He doesn't have a job. He'll be homeless, and I can't live with that."

- "I have no choice about giving my daughter money if I want to see my grandchildren."

- "I have no choice about driving my son around. He's got three DUIs and doesn't have a license anymore."

- "I don't have a choice about using my savings to pay the kids' mortgage. They love that house. They just can't afford it, and they'd so upset with me if they had to move."

- "I don't have a choice about paying for treatment, because my daughter got involved with the wrong crowd and drugs."

These parents have been trapped by the Great Lie of *no choice* because they believe the proof of being a good parent is unconditional love that supports, endorses, and enables every choice their children make, regardless of the impact on themselves and others. These are parents of physically and intellectually healthy adult children who have reached an age where it's reasonable to expect them to be self-supporting, independent, contributing members of society. These are parents who are trapped by the absolute of unconditional love, leaving themselves feeling as though they have *no choice* and can't set limits and boundaries or enforce consequences for the choices their adult children are making.

The hardest questions I ask these parents are invariably, "What will happen to your child when you're gone? Where will they live? Who will support them? How will they get by unless they are forced to learn to cope like everyone other adult?" And inevitably the responses I get are, "But what other choice do I have? How can I choose to let them stumble and fall? How can I choose to let them fail? How can I choose to see them suffer?" The answer to all of the questions they ask me is always, "How can you not, when the *no choice* enabling in which you've been engaged is hurting everyone?"

So, at the risk of being repetitive, I'll say it again: Whether we like it or not, we always choose. We choose when we act, and we choose when we don't act. Since we have no choice about *no choice*, we must face our choices head-on, make them, and act on them, for the sake of our selfhood and the potential selfhood of others.

You must enter the battle between the lies large and small, the lies Great and Personal, for control of your self and who you are. This is the battle for selfhood, the battle for whether you'll live in freedom out of your own truth or in the slavery and misery of lies. This is the battle in which we all must engage in order to live as the Heroes of our own lives.

We must find the courage to cross the threshold from the unreal, inauthentic known created by the lies that

NO CHOICE

have enslaved us and into a new, authentic known that is informed by our own truth. In the words of John Wayne, an American Hero, "Courage is being scared to death, but saddling up anyway." For when we find the courage and ride bravely into battle against the lies, we can emerge and return victorious to our own lives.

We return resurrected—reborn—to our own truth and the wisdom and freedom to understand and inform our past, present, and future so that we don't allow ourselves to be enslaved by lies, Great and Personal, ever again.

The lies, Great and Personal. Great. And Personal?

Yes, we explored the Great Lies. But the Personal Lies? What are those?

CHAPTER VI

THE PERSONAL LIES

Isn't it funny how we live inside the lies we believe?
— A. S. KING

The Great Lies are the universal lies that develop as a result of culture and the larger societal values that infuse and inform everything and everyone around us from our earliest experiences and memories. So if the Great Lies are universal, then the Personal Lies are the lies that come to us most directly from our parents and caregivers, our elders and teachers, our personal "authorities." The Personal Lies are just that—personal. They are a reflection of our personal histories as well as the histories of our personal "authorities."

We all have personal "authorities," or the people we look to for knowledge of the world around us. They are the people we looked to for the "truth" before we were old enough to venture into the world to find our own truth. Our personal "authorities" give us answers, explanations, rules, and guidelines that we believe without question, because these personal "authorities" are our very own walking, talking fountains of "truth."

Sometimes our personal "authorities" don't have as much influence as the traumas that many people suffer during their lives. People can suffer emotional, physical, or sexual abuse that distorts their thinking and prevents them from making sense of senseless things and finding a way to heal from the trauma. In these cases, our personal "authorities" are themselves unable to understand or help us heal from trauma.

The problem is that our personal "authorities" all have their own "truths" that reflect their own personally biased perspectives on and experiences of life and the world. Those biased perspectives—those biased "truths"—are passed along to us. Our personal "authorities" give their biased perspectives to us because they don't know those perspectives are biased. They don't know that their "truths" are lies any more than we do.

Our personal "authorities" pass on their knowledge, wisdom, and biased "truth" out of a desire to do the best they can for us; and in doing the best they can, they give us their biased, distorted thoughts too. These are the Personal Lies: distorted, often irrational thoughts and beliefs that we unknowingly reinforce over time. Personal Lies are what the world of mental health care calls *cognitive distortions*.

The Personal Lies, or cognitive distortions, come in many forms, but they all have three things in common:

- All Personal Lies are tendencies or patterns of thinking or believing.
- All Personal Lies are false or inaccurate.
- All Personal Lies have the potential to cause mental or emotional harm.

If you're human, you've likely fallen for a few cognitive distortions at one time or another. The difference between people who occasionally stumble into cognitive distortions and people who struggle with them over the long term is each person's ability to identify and modify or correct the lies at the heart of those faulty patterns of thinking. And those lies, those errors in thinking, are particularly effective at provoking or exacerbating the feelings that make us miserable.

Much of what we know about cognitive distortions comes from Aaron Beck and David Burns, two researchers at the forefront of the field of psychiatry and psychotherapy. Beck in particular is regarded as the father of cognitive therapy, since he was the first to identify and explain cognitive distortions as well as the ways in which people could challenge them. He found that individuals suffering mental distress often experienced streams of negative thoughts that seemed to pop into their minds automatically, and that these automatic negative thoughts fell into three categories: negative ideas about oneself, negative ideas about the world, and negative thoughts about one's future. He also believed that the limited time most people spent reflecting on (or reality testing) these automatic thoughts would lead individuals to treat those thoughts as valid or "true" when they clearly were not. Most importantly, Beck discovered that helping people to identify, understand, and challenge these automatic negative thoughts often led to the resolution of their distress.

Similarly, David Burns might be regarded as Beck's heir apparent. He extended and expanded on Beck's ideas, bringing them to the general public in his two bestselling books: *Feeling Good: The New Mood Therapy* and *The Feeling Good Handbook*. Together, these two men, as well as countless other researchers, have identified the sixteen most common cognitive distortions—the Personal Lies—that contribute to mental distress and suffering:

1. All-or-Nothing Thinking: Also known as black-and-white thinking, this Personal Lie is largely an inability or unwillingness to see shades of gray. In other words, you see things in terms of extremes. For example, something is either fantastic or awful, or you're either perfect or a total failure.

2. Overgeneralization: This sneaky Personal Lie takes one instance or example and turns it into an overall pattern. For example, a student may receive a C on one test and conclude that she is stupid and a failure. Overgeneralizing can lead to overly negative thoughts about oneself and one's environment based on only one or two experiences.

3. Mental Filter: Similar to overgeneralization, this Personal Lie focuses on a single negative and excludes all of the positives. An example of this is when one partner in a romantic relationship dwells on a single negative comment made by the other partner, then views the relationship as hopelessly lost while ignoring the years of positive comments and experiences. The mental filter can foster a negative view of everything around you by focusing only on the negative.

4. Disqualifyng the Positive: On the flip side, this Personal Lie acknowledges positive experiences but rejects them instead of embracing them. A person who receives a positive review at work may reject the idea that he is a competent employee and attribute the positive review to political correctness or to

THE PERSONAL LIES

his boss's desire to avoid discussing his employee's performance problems. This is an especially malignant Personal Lie, since it can facilitate the continuance of negative thought patterns even in the face of evidence to the contrary.

5. Jumping to Conclusions—Mind Reading: This Personal Lie is the inaccurate belief that we know what another person is thinking. Of course, it's possible to have an idea of what other people are thinking, but this lie refers to the negative interpretations that we jump to. Seeing a stranger with an unpleasant expression and jumping to the conclusion that she is thinking something negative about you is an example of this.

6. Jumping to Conclusions—Fortune-Telling: A sister lie to mind reading, fortune-telling is the tendency to make conclusions and predictions based on little to no evidence and holding them as gospel truth. One example is a young, single woman predicting that she will never find love or have a committed and happy relationship based only on the fact that she hasn't found it yet. There is simply no way for her to know how her life will turn out, but she sees this prediction as fact rather than one of several possible outcomes.

7. Magnification (Catastrophizing) or Minimization: Also known as the binocular trick for its stealthy skewing of your perspective, this Personal Lie involves exaggerating or minimizing the importance

or meaning of things. An athlete who is generally a good player but makes a mistake may magnify the importance of that mistake and believe he is a terrible teammate, while an athlete who wins a coveted award in her sport may minimize the importance of the award and continue believing she is only a mediocre player.

8. Emotional Reasoning: This may be one of the most surprising Personal Lies. It's also one of the most important lies to identify and address. Emotional reasoning refers to the acceptance of one's emotions as fact. It can be described as, "I feel it. Therefore, it must be true." Of course, we know this isn't a reasonable belief, but it's a common one nonetheless.

9. "Should" Statements: Another particularly damaging Personal Lie is the tendency to make "should" statements. These are statements you make to yourself about what you think you should, ought to, or must do. They can also be applied to others, imposing a set of expectations that will likely not be met. When we hang on too tightly to our "should" statements about ourselves, the result is often guilt that we can't live up to those statements. When we cling to our "should" statements about others, we're generally disappointed by the failure of the others to meet our expectations, leading to anger and resentment.

10. Labeling and Mislabeling: These tendencies are extreme forms of overgeneralization in which we assign judgments of value to ourselves or to others

THE PERSONAL LIES

based on one instance or experience. For example, a student who labels herself as "an utter fool" for failing an assignment is engaging in this Personal Lie, as is the waiter who labels a customer "a grumpy old miser" if he fails to thank the waiter for bringing his food. Mislabeling refers to the application of highly emotional, loaded language when labeling.

11. Personalization: As the name implies, this Personal Lie involves taking everything personally or assigning blame to yourself with no logical reason to believe you're to blame. This lie covers a wide range of situations, from assuming you're the reason a friend didn't enjoy the girls' night out because of you, to believing you're the cause for every instance of moodiness or irritation in those around you.

12. Control Fallacy: A control fallacy presents itself as one of two beliefs: (1) we have no control over our lives and are helpless victims of fate; or (2) we're in complete control of ourselves and our surroundings, which gives us responsibility for the feelings of those around us. Both lies are damaging and inaccurate. No one is in complete control of what happens to them, and no one has absolutely no control over their situation. Even in extreme situations where an individual seemingly has no choices in what they do, where they go, or what they say, they still have a certain amount of control over how they approach their situation mentally.

13. Fallacy of Fairness: While we would all probably prefer to operate in a world that is fair, this as-

sumption isn't based in reality and can foster negative feelings when we're faced with proof of life's unfairness. A person who judges every experience by its perceived fairness has fallen for this Personal Lie and will likely feel anger, resentment, and hopelessness when he inevitably encounters a situation that isn't fair.

14. Fallacy of Change: This Personal Lie involves expecting others to change if we pressure or encourage them enough. It's usually accompanied by a belief that our happiness and success rests on other people, leading us to believe that forcing those around us to change is the only way to get what we want. If a man thinks, *If I just encourage my wife to stop doing the things that irritate me, I can be a better husband and a happier person*, he is exhibiting the fallacy of change.

15. Always Being Right: Perfectionists and those struggling with imposter syndrome will recognize this Personal Lie. It's the belief that we must always be right, correct, or accurate. With this lie, the idea that we could be wrong is absolutely unacceptable, and we'll fight to the metaphorical death to prove that we're right. For example, the internet commenters who spend hours arguing with each other over an opinion or political issue far beyond the point where reasonable individuals would conclude that they should "agree to disagree" are engaging in this Personal Lie. To them, it's not simply a matter of a difference of opinion. It's an intellectual battle that must be won at all costs.

THE PERSONAL LIES

16. Heaven's Reward Fallacy: This Personal Lie is a popular one, particularly with the myriad examples of this fallacy playing out on big and small screens across the world. It's the belief that one's struggles, suffering, and hard work will result in a just reward. It's obvious why this type of thinking is a lie. How many examples can you think of, just within the realm of your personal acquaintances, where hard work and sacrifice didn't pay off? Sometimes, no matter how hard we work or how much we sacrifice, we won't achieve what we hope to achieve. To think otherwise is a potentially damaging pattern of thought that can result in disappointment, frustration, anger, and even depression when the awaited reward doesn't materialize.

You may recognize many of these Personal Lies because, like all of us, you are human and have allowed one or more of these Personal Lies to influence you, enslave you, create distress, and torture you. You learned these Personal Lies early and embraced them as truth because you didn't know any better. You didn't know how to recognize them or challenge them because they were the automatic negative thoughts that had become the whole cloth of your internal dialogue and emotional "reality." You didn't know that you could do something—anything—to free yourself from the slavery of Personal Lies.

But you can.

You can learn to recognize and challenge these lies, then replace them with your own authentic truth. You can create a new cloth, a new you.

You can reclaim your selfhood and live a life of your

own, informed by your own truth and wisdom, so that you can become the Hero of your own life.

You can embark on the Hero's Journey.

CHAPTER VII

THE HERO'S JOURNEY

*If there is no one to challenge the
lie, it becomes a new Truth.*
— **BIMAN GHANDI**

There are many ways to challenge the lies and learn the truth. However, they all begin with the Hero's Journey.

As mentioned in the introduction, I first came across the idea of the Hero's Journey in the works of Joseph Campbell, an American mythologist, writer, and lecturer who is best known for his work in comparative mythology and comparative religion. His work covers many aspects of the human experience, and his philosophy is often summarized by this phrase: "Follow your bliss."

In his first book, *The Hero with a Thousand Faces*, Campbell proposed a universal pattern that is the essence of heroic tales in every culture. While outlining the basic stages of this mythic cycle, he also explores common variations in the Hero's Journey, which, he argues, is a metaphor not only for an individual, but for a culture as well. While the Hero's Journey has been described by many people over time in many different ways, all of the tellings contain common elements.

In the beginning, the Hero (or protagonist) lives in the ordinary world and receives the call to enlightenment and selfhood. The Hero is often reluctant to follow the

THE HERO'S JOURNEY

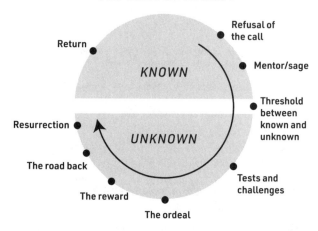

call because of the dangers and hardships that threaten. At this point, the Hero may be aided by a sage or mentor. The Hero begins by making the choice to go forward and traverse the threshold to the unknown, where the Hero faces tasks or trials either alone or with the assistance of helpers. Eventually the Hero reaches "the innermost cave," or the central crisis of the adventure, where they must undergo "the ordeal" and overcome the main obstacle or enemy, thus undergoing "a change" and gaining their reward (a treasure or "elixir"). The Hero must then return to the ordinary world with the reward. The Hero may be pursued by the guardians of the unknown—or they may be reluctant to return and then must be rescued or forced to return by intervention from the outside. In the return, the Hero again traverses the threshold, returning to the ordinary world with the treasure or elixir gained, which the Hero may now use for the benefit of their fellow man.

THE HERO'S JOURNEY

The Hero is also transformed by the adventure and gains wisdom or spiritual power over both worlds.

By believing and accepting a lie such as *no choice*, we're knowingly and willingly enslaving ourselves to a lie. And to free ourselves and achieve selfhood, we all must make the choice to embark on the Hero's Journey.

For each of us on the journey, we're living in the ordinary world, going about our ordinary lives, when we receive a call, that quiet voice inside all of us that speaks to our deepest hopes and desires. That quiet voice tells us we need or want something more, something different, something real and authentic to our selfhood. We're often reluctant to listen to that call out of fear of the unknown; fear that we may be overcome or overwhelmed by the "monsters" we may need to face; fear of the loss of something, someone, or an idea we've cherished; or fear that answering that call will change us and everything we know.

The first words out of Cindy's mouth when we met in my office for the first time were, "I didn't want to come here today." Cindy was a wife, mother, and teacher in her fifties who had enjoyed a good life but, like many of us, still felt unhappy and unsatisfied. She described having friends, interests, and an active, involved life; and that she had struggled for years with depression and anxiety. "I've got no real reason to feel this way, and I'm a smart person, so I should be able to figure this out," she had said. "I'm not sure I even believe in therapy. I just know I have to figure some things out and do something different."

Cindy had heard the call of that small, quiet voice that told her she needed and wanted something more, something different. She had been reluctant to listen to that call for years out of fear of what it might entail, what she might need to face, and what she might need to do. As it turned out, there was a "monster" in Cindy's closet that she had been afraid to face and challenge. She needed to embark on the Hero's Journey, but she was unsure about how to do that. So she found the courage to walk into a therapist's office despite the fact that she "didn't want to come here today." Cindy took her Hero's Journey, faced down and defeated her "monster," and returned to her life—and her world changed. And by doing so, Cindy became the Hero of her own life.

For some of us, like Cindy, we may be aided by a sage or mentor of some kind—a leader, a book, a teacher, a therapist—who helps us to understand and find the courage to move forward and cross the threshold into the unknown. Crossing the threshold means moving from the known—the way it's always been, the lies we've always "known" and accepted—into the unknown, where we face and challenge the monsters and the lies that have enslaved us and kept us in misery.

When we answer the call and cross the threshold from the known into the unknown, we move into our transformation. In other words, we move toward personal freedom and selfhood. We move into a space where we recognize, challenge, and free ourselves from the lies that have enslaved and controlled us.

Our transformation is literally action packed, although the action takes place largely within ourselves. We'll discuss this at length later in this book, when we describe and examine the ways in which we can do the work of recognizing, challenging, and freeing ourselves from lies and achieving authentic selfhood. For now, suffice it to say that our transformation involves tests from and challenges to the "moral authority" as well as the "unquestionable" values of the societal, familial, and personal cultures in which we were raised. These tests and challenges lead to an ordeal, which is the climax of our transformation and where we must face everything we've always "known" and have been told to be true, and fight for ourselves and what we believe to be the truth of ourselves and our own lives.

This ordeal is the final battle between you and the lies, Great and Personal, for control of your self and who you are. This is the battle for selfhood, the battle for whether you'll live in freedom out of your own truth or in the slavery and misery of lies. This is the battle in which we all must engage in order to live as the Hero of our own life.

Do you remember Phillip, the "diseased and deformed" twenty-eight-year-old man who had been trapped by the Great Lie of *I can't*? His transformation tests and challenges included learning to manage ulcerative colitis and finding appropriate ways to exercise without damaging his feet. But Phillip's final ordeal involved creating healthy boundaries with his mother, his wife, and other important people in his life, which allowed him to become everything he could be and find his authentic self. In that way, Phillip became the Hero of his own life.

Having fought this battle and won, we move into the return. In this final stage, we receive our reward, claim our authentic selfhood, and return with our newfound wisdom and freedom to transform our "ordinary" lives into the ones we've always wanted, needed, and deserved. We cross the threshold once more from the unknown into a new, authentic known that's informed by our own truth. We return resurrected—reborn—to our own truth and the wisdom and freedom to understand and inform our past, present, and future so that we don't allow ourselves to be enslaved by the lies, Great and Personal, ever again.

So how do we begin our own Hero's Journey? How do we answer the call? Find a mentor or sage? Cross the threshold from the known into the unknown? Face the tests and challenges at the center of the unknown? Triumph over the ordeal? Win the reward of our own authentic truth? And return to our everyday lives reborn as the Hero of our own life?

At this point, you may be asking, "Can I do it on my own? Or do I need help?"

Help is always good. But what kind of help do we need to complete our Hero's Journey? What kind of mentor or sage will help us to find the courage to face the tests and challenges, stand up to the lies Great and Personal, and become the Hero of our own lives?

There are many potential answers to these questions that will be explored later in this book. However, let's begin with what our culture as well as science and industry would have us believe.

Let's begin with the lie that there is magic in a pill.

CHAPTER VIII

THE MAGIC IN A PILL

There are two ways to be fooled. One is to believe what isn't true; the other is to refuse to believe what is true.
— **SØREN KIERKEGAARD**

Until 1950, the predominant theories about how the brain works were electrical, not chemical. Since the 1950s, a range of medical specialists, pharmaceutical companies, cultural critics, and journalists have been trying to convince us that medications can restore selfhood—to believe that there is magic in a pill.

It was the discovery of numerous researchers that the tranquilizer reserpine seemed to cause depression and even suicide in some users, which suggested a biological basis for depression. Reserpine is one of the hormones in the brain that acts as a messenger between brain cells; and in the normal course of relaying messages between brain cells, reserpine depletes the brain of neurotransmitters called monoamines. When reserpine causes levels of monoamines to decrease, it produces a decline in activity that, to the researchers, looked like a depressed person's lower energy level and lack of initiative. Seeming to confirm this reasoning was the concurrent discovery of two types of antidepressant medication that increased monoamine activity. Depression, it seemed, might be a relatively simple biological disorder caused by incorrect levels of a few chemicals in the brain.

This biogenesis theory had enormous appeal for nearly everyone concerned with mental illness, from suffering individuals, to physicians and researchers, to pharmaceutical and insurance companies. It potentially freed people from the stigma of mental illness by characterizing depression as a biochemical malfunction like diabetes and promising a simple "cure" with the ease of medication. For the majority of physicians who were increasingly facing patients presenting what had been previously characterized as "psychological" problems, identifying a biochemical basis for their suffering meant that they could now treat these patients "medically." In addition, depression as a neurochemical imbalance gave researchers a clear and specific direction to identify the chemical combinations, most notably selective serotonin reuptake inhibitors (SSRIs) and selective norepinephrine reuptake inhibitors (SNRIs), that could rebalance a person out of depression.

It was the introduction of Prozac in 1987 and Peter Kramer's book *Listening to Prozac: A Psychiatrist Explores Antidepressant Drugs and the Remaking of the Self* that catapulted the lie of the magic in a pill to a culturally accepted value. In a widely quoted passage from his book, Kramer, a psychiatrist, stated that Prozac had the ability to make patients "better than well," pointing toward a new era in which "cosmetic psychopharmacology" would allow people to sculpt socially attractive personalities. In other words, the drug could not only cure illness, but also allow individuals to manipulate their identity, the essence of themselves.

Prozac appeared to validate the biogenesis theory of mental distress and suffering. In 1999, US Surgeon General David Satcher stated unequivocally that "[t]he bases of mental illness are chemical changes in the brain. . . . [T]here is no longer any justification for the distinction . . . between 'mind and body' or 'mental and physical illnesses.' Mental illnesses are physical illnesses."

Prozac and its subsequent psychoactive siblings could now be likened to a whole host of other medications that could "rebalance" a person's neurological requirements, much like insulin "rebalanced" the diabetic. These technological medical miracles were widely prescribed and reported as effective in treating depression, anxiety, smoking cessation, bipolar symptoms, menstrual distress, stomach distress, skin rashes, insomnia, alcoholism, obsessive-compulsive behavior, juvenile behavior disorders, cardiovascular disorders, preoperative and postoperative conditions, dermatologic ailments, allergic conditions, gastrointestinal disturbances, and menopausal hot flashes.

What helped make Prozac and its successors so successful was the concept of selectivity. This concept suggested that these drugs would permit control of the brain so precisely as to give individuals the choice of a custom-made self and achieve the desired effects without any unwanted changes in other areas of the body, brain, or personality. These "planfully" constructed medicines would restore or enhance individuals to their true selves and allow achievement of the life it was presumed everyone wanted.

All this isn't to say that these drugs didn't relieve the very real suffering that some people experience. These medications did then—and still do—help the most severely depressed and anxious, the 2 to 3 percent of us that are simply overwhelmed by a debilitating disease they can't manage. However, these drugs were—and are—the most widely prescribed medications available, being prescribed for anywhere from 25 to 50 percent of the population, according to the National Institutes of Health. The vast majority of people taking these drugs were not—and are not—the severely depressed and anxious, but rather the people who are plagued and enslaved by thoughts that keep them from living the lives they have always wanted and deserved to live.

Interestingly, research into the effectiveness of these new wonder drugs began almost as soon as they were prescribed. In the early 1990s, scientific journals and popular media alike were flooded with reports of the effectiveness of SSRIs and SNRIs. However, by the mid- to late 1990s, other reports began to surface suggesting that claims of effectiveness may have been an empty promise. The latest research on the effectiveness of SSRIs and SNRIs, particularly meta-analytic evaluations that look at many research studies all at once, increasingly indicate that the effectiveness of these medications isn't significantly different from that of a placebo. Specifically, the true drug effects for these medications have been found to be nonexistent or negligible among people with mild, moderate, and even severe symptoms. Only among the most severely affected have these medications been found to be effective to a significant degree.

Speculation regarding the apparent reversal of scientific data in support of these medications' effectiveness has identified a number of possible reasons, including how researchers measure distress and relief from distress;

selective publication bias where research that doesn't support the researcher's beliefs is never published; financial incentives to researchers from drug manufacturers, which influence research outcomes; how even taking a placebo may be perceived by an individual as "doing something" to address their difficulties and is therefore helpful; and that the chemical imbalance/biogenesis theory is simply wrong. All these factors may contribute (to a greater or lesser extent) to the developing body of knowledge and belief that medications appear to be minimally effective at best in the treatment of most forms of depression and anxiety.

Let's take a deeper look at what the latest research is telling us about the chemical imbalance/biogenesis theory. We've been told that these medications work by adjusting neurochemical transmitters in the brain that are believed to be connected to depressive and anxious symptoms. However, due to brain plasticity—the ability of the brain to change, adapt, and keep everything in balance—some researchers have suggested that artificial up-and-down regulation of neurochemicals by a medication is compensated for within the brain naturally, thereby negating any pharmacological effect of these drugs. In other words, your brain is always working to keep everything in balance; and when you add more serotonin or norepinephrine through a drug, the brain tells the body to stop making so much serotonin or norepinephrine. Therefore, the drugs do nothing to impact the distress that people are experiencing.

This may explain why many people suffering from distress will often report a return of symptoms within twelve to eighteen months of beginning one of these medications.

More importantly, even though new drugs must undergo clinical trials in order to receive FDA approval, there are no requirements regarding the length of the trial or follow-up; and most trials of antidepressant drugs range from only four to eight weeks. That's a far shorter time than most people take these medications and likely a far shorter time than the brain requires to balance itself. This may also explain why there has been an upsurge in ads telling users of these medications that "if you're not getting the relief you need from your existing antidepressant, ask your doctor to add [insert name of medication]," encouraging sufferers to take yet another medication.

However, these drugs are doing something to the people who are taking them, particularly among those who are taking them for long periods of time. In 2008, the American Medical Association warned physicians that individuals who were taking antidepressant medications—which were originally described as nonhabit-forming—could be subject to what has been termed *antidepressant discontinuation syndrome*. This syndrome is estimated to affect from 20 to 80 percent of people who are taking antidepressants and involves physical and emotional impacts that may make these drugs difficult to discontinue.

Similarly, a variety of physical side effects have emerged beyond those identified when these medications were first introduced. Among people taking these medications for long periods of time, a variety of recent studies including meta-analyses, longitudinal studies, and randomized controlled trials have found that these medications appear to be correlated with increased development of osteoporosis in women, increased bone fracture risk in older adults, increased fall risk in older adults, increased

DNA fragmentation and decreased fertility in men, an increased risk of developing type 2 diabetes when used in combination with older antidepressant medications, and an increased risk of sudden cardiac death. It appears as though the risks of these medications may outweigh the reported benefits.

So, is all this a way to say that for people suffering with mental distress, medication is *not* the help they need? That they *shouldn't* take these medications? That these medications do nothing to aid people in their fight against the lies that enslave them?

Not necessarily.

What these medications can do for some people is to temporarily make room in their heads for recognizing and challenging the lies that bind them to misery. They can also provide more mental energy temporarily, help lift the fog that clouds people's thinking, and help people sleep better, eat better, or cry less so they can focus better on understanding and identifying what is making them miserable and then do something about it.

Many of the people I've worked with over the years started out by talking to their doctor about the symptoms of anxiety and depression they were experiencing, and their doctor started them on an antidepressant or anti-anxiety medication. Most of these people were hopeful that they had found "the answer," that the medication prescribed for them would make their depression or anxiety go away—only to discover three months, six months, or two years down the road that, while they had gotten some temporary relief from their symptoms, generally they were still feeling as depressed or anxious as ever. These people found their way to me because the promise of the "magic in a pill" was as empty as many of them were feeling.

It's also important to clarify that medications are critically important for some forms of mental distress, most notably the bipolar and schizophrenia spectrum disorders. These disorders have been proven repeatedly, and over many decades, to have a biochemical component that can only be managed with the help of medication. Without medications, people suffering with these disorders can experience distress that leads to a host of difficulties, including severe depression, mania, loss of contact with reality, drug abuse, jail and/or prison time, despair, and even death. Medications designed to treat the bipolar and schizophrenia spectrum disorders are necessary for suffering individuals to manage the biochemical basis of the illness and provide them the mental relief that's critical to challenging the lies in their heads.

Whether medications work temporarily for most forms of distress or over the long term for bipolar and schizophrenia spectrum disorders, the common factor that's absolutely and unequivocally necessary to freeing ourselves from the slavery of lies is learning to recognize, challenge, and change those lies. Although we may find a "magic" sword, shield, or elixir, we must first and foremost face, challenge, and overcome our demons—our lies—by reaching deep inside and fighting with the strength and courage that resides in us.

And the first step to reaching inside to overcome our lies—the first step on the Hero's Journey—is hearing, listening to, and answering the call.

"Okay," you may be saying. "So what's the big deal? I hear things all the time. I have to listen to all kinds of stuff. Why the fuss about hearing, listening, and answering? Don't we all do this all the time, whether we want to or not?"

Well, the answer to all of these questions is yes and no. Yes, we all hear all kinds of things all the time. Hearing is one of our senses—basically, your ears performing their function of receiving sound waves and noise. Listening is a step further than hearing; it implies that, after the brain receives the nerve impulses and deciphers the sound or noise, the brain assigns a meaning or level of importance to what it hears and sends feedback. Listening is different from hearing because it requires more conscious action. The main difference between hearing and listening is the amount of attention put into it. Hearing simply happens, whereas listening requires concentration and effort. Human beings can hear sounds much faster than they can process thoughts. In a world with so many different background noises, humans have developed the ability to block out certain sounds and only focus on certain things. In other words—and as we all know—it's possible to hear without listening.

Hearing without listening is what happens when we refuse or reject the call, since we don't answer it. The call can be refused, rejected, or left unanswered for many reasons. However, when it comes to facing and challenging the lies that have enslaved us and created so much of our misery and distress, the reason for refusing or rejecting the call is likely related to where we are in something called the stages of change.

CHAPTER IX

THE STAGES OF CHANGE

*The truth is messy. It's raw and uncomfortable.
You can't blame people for preferring lies.*
— **HOLLY BLACK**

The stages of change model is a framework that describes the series of stages or steps we go through to change ourselves, our lives, and our habits, including habitual thinking patterns and behaviors. This model was originally developed by James Prochaska and Carlo DiClemente in the late 1970s through a series of studies comparing the experiences of smokers who quit on their own versus those unable to quit on their own in order to understand the differences between the two groups. Prochaska and DiClemente determined that people could quit smoking on their own only *if they were ready to do so.*

Sounds simple and obvious, doesn't it? If you're ready to do something, then you can do it. But what Prochaska and DiClemente discovered was anything but simple and obvious. It was an entire series of internal processes we all go through before, during, and after we make any kind of change in our lives.

Although the stages of change model was originally developed to better understand how smokers are able to give up their addiction to cigarettes, it has since been used to understand changing just about any type of behavior, including our thinking. The critical assumption that underpins this model is that change doesn't happen in one step, but through a series of distinct, predictable stages; and just realizing the stage of change you're in may be helpful for you to succeed.

Studies have found that people move through a series of stages when modifying their behavior. While the time a person can stay in each stage is variable, the tasks required to move to the next stage are not. Certain principles and processes of change work best at each stage to reduce resistance, facilitate progress, and prevent relapse.

The stages of change model suggests certain change-related thoughts and behaviors unfold as a process over time, progressing through a series of stages. While progression through the stages of change can occur in a linear fashion, a nonlinear progression is common, meaning that individuals often recycle through the stages or regress to earlier stages from later ones.

The Stages of Change

THE STAGES OF CHANGE

PRECONTEMPLATION: "NO, NOT ME"

People in this first stage don't want to make any changes and don't recognize that they have a problem. This is an "ignorance is bliss" stage; in precontemplation, individuals may be pessimistic about their ability to make changes. They may even deny the negative effects of their existing habits, or their pervasive Great and Personal lies. They selectively filter information that helps confirm their decision not to question or challenge anything they have been taught or told. This stage is many times referred to as the denial stage. Unfortunately, people in the precontemplation stage appear unable to hear the call or may reject hearing the call. It often takes an emotional trigger or event of some kind to snap people out of this stage.

We all know friends, relatives, and other people who are in the precontemplation stage. They are the folks who have a drinking problem but think they just need to unwind. They are the ones who keep choosing partners other people think are mean, manipulative, or untrustworthy, but who view those partners as just troubled, misunderstood, or people who "haven't found the right person." They are the ones who are hard to get along with because they always have to be right, and who think they have just had a lot of bad luck in working for terrible bosses.

CONTEMPLATION: "WELL, MAYBE . . ."

During this second stage, you're sitting on the proverbial fence, weighing the costs and benefits of change. You're contemplating whether the change will be worth it. You may recognize that your thoughts and choices are problematic; a more thoughtful and practical consideration of the pros and cons of changing takes place, with equal emphasis placed on both sides. Even with this recognition, though, people may still feel ambivalent toward change and can remain in this stage for years without preparing to take action. If you can identify new ways that making a change will benefit you, the benefits will outweigh the costs. People tend to seek pleasure and avoid pain, so the more pleasure you can ascribe to making a change, the more likely you'll take action and succeed.

In the three examples above, the changes in thought and behavior generally go like this:

- "Lately, it seems like all my friends tell me I drink too much. Some of them say I'm even kind of obnoxious when I drink. I don't think I drink too much, and I'm not sure I want to stop drinking. I'm not obnoxious; I'm fun-loving. Still, they are my friends, and I probably should listen to them."

- "Nobody ever wants to get together with us as couples anymore, because they don't like my boyfriend. But they never like any of my boyfriends. They think every guy I get involved with is a user or a loser. It's true that I seem to meet a lot of guys who have a lot of trouble in their lives or who want something from me—and the last few relationships haven't ended well. I really like this new guy, though, and I think he just needs to be with somebody who isn't a psycho. I know I've said that before, so maybe I should figure this out before I get hurt again."

- "Just my luck that I got another boss who won't listen to me, but it seems like that's the only kind of boss I get. My kids say I can't get along with anyone because

I'm the one who doesn't listen. I know I'm right about this, but I keep running into this, and I'm not getting the promotions I deserve. Maybe I need to do something about it."

PREPARATION: "WHAT DO I DO NOW?"

People in the preparation stage have decided to change their negative habits and are planning in very specific and concrete ways how they will make a change. They are testing the waters, so to speak, and will start to take small steps toward thought and behavior changes, because they believe changing their thinking and behavior can lead to a better life. People who are in this stage are asking friends and family what they might do. They may be looking for help from a therapist, Alcoholics Anonymous (AA), or a job coach; or they may be exploring courses online. These individuals are identifying resources and weighing their options in order to take the next step.

ACTION: "LET'S DO THIS"

The action stage is the process of changing your life by changing your thinking and your choices. In this stage, you've recently changed your thinking, and you intend to keep moving forward with that change. The action stage is when the people in our examples get into a chemical dependency treatment program and join AA, find a self-help book or therapist that helps them change their thinking and choices in relationships, or start working with a job coach or online course to learn how to engage in collaborative interactions with others.

MAINTENANCE: "IT IS POSSIBLE!"

This is the stage of successful, sustained life change. However, individuals in this stage are also at the greatest risk of relapse, so it's key to leverage any techniques that work for you to stay motivated. People in this stage work to prevent relapse into one of the earlier stages.

In terms of the lies that bind, the Great and the Personal, most of the world lives in the precontemplation stage, or the rejection of the call. Precontemplation is, "I'm fine. There's nothing wrong with me. If everybody else would just [fill in the blank with your situation], I'd be perfectly happy." When people are in the precontemplation stage, they lack motivation, desire, and drive, and are unlikely to do what they have to do to become the Hero of their own life.

On the Hero's Journey, the contemplation and preparation stages are about finding a sage or mentor and crossing the threshold from the known to the unknown in order to begin recognizing and challenging the lies, Great and Personal, that have been the source of your suffering. Individuals who are in these stages are willing to open their minds and themselves to possibilities and questions in both large and small ways. These are the people who are challenging the lies, and are learning to ask questions such as "Why?" and "Why not?" and "What if?"

In the Action stage, we identify our Great and Personal lies, what makes them lies, and how they have enslaved us and created our distress. Individuals in this stage are rejecting the lies that have been imposed on them and have enslaved them. They are slaying the monsters in the

THE STAGES OF CHANGE

closet. People who are in the Action stage are filling their thoughts, feelings, choices, and behaviors with their own authentic truth. These individuals are facing the ordeal of changing lies for truth, even when the truth they speak and live is challenged by others. They have embraced their truth, their authentic selfhood, and the reward of becoming the Hero of their own life.

Finally, in the Maintenance stage, the Hero returns, resurrected and reborn, to the ordinary world to carry selfhood and authentic truth forward into every part of their life. As I mentioned earlier, maintenance is the stage at which we're at the greatest risk for falling back into our old habitual thinking and becoming enslaved by lies again. We're at risk largely because our recognition and rejection of lies is often threatening to others who are still enslaved by their lies. We've all heard that misery loves company. Well, lies love company too, and will attack anyone and anything that tries to call them out for what they are.

Maintenance is the stage in which we may be challenged by friends, family, coworkers, and others—even ourselves and our old thinking habits—because we're no longer the person we used to be and the person they are familiar and comfortable with. We no longer think, believe, or behave in the same way. We have changed, but others haven't—and they might not like the way in which we've changed. And so our friends, family, and coworkers may try to force us back into the slavery of lies. This is why, during the maintenance stage, you need to keep your skills and techniques for recognizing and rejecting lies fresh and strong.

When I first met Bill, he was in his early fifties, was divorced, had three children, and was doing well in his career. Bill had come to see me because he was worried about his children. "My kids' mom isn't a bad person," he said. "She's just so into herself and her own things that she really hasn't been there for them. My oldest left town to get away from the family stuff, my middle kid is drinking way too much, and my youngest is struggling to find her own way and is worried about me. She's mostly why I'm here today." It turned out that his youngest child was worried about Bill because every night after work, Bill would drink . . . and drink . . . and drink, until he fell asleep. "It's not a problem because it doesn't affect my work, and I've never gotten a DUI or anything like that," Bill explained. He said he would drink to relax, and he didn't see it as a problem. At that point, Bill was in precontemplation.

Over the course of therapy, Bill moved into the contemplation stage and started asking himself questions about his drinking, including what he was avoiding with alcohol and the ways in which alcohol was keeping him from himself. The answers to these questions were life-changing for Bill. He became aware that he had been drinking for years out of feeling hurt by and angry with his ex-wife, as well as feeling as though hurting himself might get through to her and hurt her as well. "I know it doesn't make any sense," he said, "but it's like *I* was drinking poison and expected it to poison *her*. But all I'm doing is hurting me and my kids."

This epiphany helped move Bill from contemplation into action. Bill got into a treatment program and began attending AA. He sold the home where he had lived when he had been married and found a new place to live that felt like "him." He bought a bike, joined a gym, and used that time that had been devoted to drinking to getting

THE STAGES OF CHANGE

himself healthy again. Bill gave up hurt and anger in favor of becoming the Hero of his own life—and, along the way, a Hero to his children.

There is also the temptation during the maintenance stage to try to force others to begin their own Hero's Journey. Having achieved maintenance, most of us will feel so good and free that we want to share this with those we care about. We want to free them from the slavery of lies, Great and Personal, so they can join us in authentic selfhood and truth. But just as no one could force you to begin your journey, you can't force others to do the same, no matter how much you care for them.

Toward the end of our therapy, Bill often mused about his desire to get his son, who was still drinking too much, to find the answers and make the changes Bill had made. "I feel so good," Bill said, "and I wish I had done this years ago. I think about my son, and I don't want him to have to go through what I went through. I want to tell him everything and get him on the path too." Bill wanted to share his newfound revelations about taking the Hero's Journey in order to help his son stop drinking and become the Hero of his own life. But by being reminded to use his skills as an Objective Observer, examining the evidence, challenging his thinking, and recognizing that everyone's Hero's Journey is unique and intensely personal, Bill came to the realization that his son had to make his own Hero's Journey in his own way, at his own time.

The stages of change are a map for the Hero's Journey so we can leave behind a life of misery and distress and find truth and selfhood. To make this journey and move through the necessary stages, we must first be ready to undertake the Hero's Journey. We must hear, listen to, and answer the call. We must move out of precontemplation and recognize that we can have the lives we've dreamed of.

But how do we make the move from precontemplation to contemplation and begin our journey?

Just as hearing the call isn't listening, simply seeing isn't observing. And we must learn to observe objectively, without bias or judgment.

Seeing is also one of our senses—basically, your eyes performing their function of receiving light waves. It's passive information-gathering, an ordinary, everyday occurrence. Observing is a step further than seeing, because observing is active and objectivity is intentional and powerful—and critically important.

Becoming an Objective Observer is the first step on the Hero's Journey.

CHAPTER X

THE OBJECTIVE OBSERVER

People trust their eyes above all else—but most people see what they wish to see, or what they believe they should see; not what is really there.
— ZOË MARRIOTT

Have you ever noticed how much easier it is to see and understand the answers to other people's problems than it is to see and understand the answers to your own? Or to know what would fix or help whatever is troubling your friend, significant other, sister, or child, but they just don't seem to see it?

I often tell people I work with that, as a psychotherapist, I have the easiest job in the world. People come to see me, and I listen to their stories, make observations about what is troubling them, and recommend things they could do to fix it. But I don't actually do anything other than be an Objective Observer. My job is to hear what they have to say without judgement, assumptions, or preconceived ideas about them or their world; to lay out the map of their world that they have drawn for me with their words, actions, and choices, then show them possible routes to their desired destination.

Being an Objective Observer means taking in or dealing with facts or conditions without distortion by personal feelings, prejudices, assumptions, or interpretations.

You're acting solely as a bystander, an onlooker, a spectator, a viewer, or a watcher. You're simply looking at, hearing, or perceiving something or someone as they most simply and obviously exist.

In his 1961 science fiction novel *Stranger in a Strange Land*, Robert Heinlein created the idea of the Fair Witness, an individual trained to be an absolutely impartial witness. Point to a white house and ask a Fair Witness what color it is, and they will tell you, "It appears to be white on this side." They won't assume, infer, interpret, or guess that the whole house is the same as the part they can see, but only report what they experience or directly witness.

For most of us, being an Objective Observer—a Fair Witness—of others is easy, because we can often recognize and put aside our personal feelings, assumptions, or prejudices and simply observe because what we're observing doesn't affect us directly. We can look at the choices and actions of our coworkers, friends, and loved ones in a more dispassionate and unbiased way than we can generally do for ourselves. Yet we must become Objective Observers of our own thoughts, feelings, and behaviors in order to overcome the lies, Great and Personal, and become the Heroes of our own lives.

Unlike becoming an Objective Observer of others, becoming an Objective Observer of ourselves and our own thoughts is one of the most difficult things for many people to do. It's human nature to interpret situations, actions, or others' words in accordance with what we "know" based on our history or our view of any situation, relationship, or dispute. For example, if your working theory is that an employee is unreliable, then you might assume he's late for a meeting because he's unreliable and disorganized.

THE OBJECTIVE OBSERVER

However, if you're late for a meeting, it's because of traffic. The simple fact of being late for a meeting is interpreted in two very different ways, simply based on the theory you bring to the table.

An interesting "scientific" example of the ways in which our personal feelings, prejudices, assumptions, or interpretations bias our thinking and judgment comes from Lawrence Kohlberg and Carol Gilligan. These well-known psychology researchers were interested in how human beings develop a moral sense or judgment, but went about their research in very different ways based on their working theories. Kohlberg developed his theory of moral development while studying male children and adolescents. Gilligan challenged Kohlberg's work through her research on moral development in young and adolescent girls.

Kohlberg's theory, based on the thinking and judgment of boys, emphasized laws and justice. Gilligan's work, based on research with girls, outlines how a woman's morality is influenced by relationships and how their decisions will affect others. Two researchers who were doing important and valid work on the same facet of human development, with two very different yet important and valid working theories, were influenced by their personal feelings, prejudices, assumptions, and interpretations.

So which one is right? It appears to depend on your perspective or working theory. Perhaps they are both right. Perhaps they are both wrong. However, it's undeniable that these two scientific researchers, who each worked to understand human thinking and behavior using well-accepted scientific research methods, were strongly influenced by their feelings, prejudices, assumptions, and interpretations and came to two very different conclusions.

In the short story "A Scandal in Bohemia," the fictional detective Sherlock Holmes makes an important point about personal feelings, prejudices, interpretations, and rushing to judgement. After reading a note from a mysterious correspondent, Sherlock's friend Dr. Watson asks Sherlock what he imagines it means. Sherlock doesn't believe in imagination, though. He believes in direct, dispassionate, objective observation. He says, "I have no data yet. It is a capital mistake to theorize before one has data. Insensibly one begins to twist facts to suit theories, instead of theories to suit facts."

An Objective Observer, like a Fair Witness or Sherlock Holmes, avoids working theories and assumptions. Yet we all have working theories and assumptions in our thinking, whether we're aware of them or not. And some of our working theories and assumptions are actually thought processes known as *heuristics*.

Heuristics are simple, efficient rules which people often use to form judgments and make decisions. They are strategies derived from previous experiences with similar problems, or mental shortcuts that involve focusing on one aspect of a complex problem and ignoring others in order to reach an immediate, short-term goal. These shortcuts may work well in many circumstances. But because they are shortcuts, they can lead to systematic deviations from logic, probability, or rational choice. The resulting errors are called *cognitive biases* and are often at the heart of Personal lies.

Heuristics usually govern automatic, intuitive judgments but can also be used as deliberate mental strategies when working from limited information. Research has identified a variety of heuristics in our thinking. For example, just because something has worked in the past doesn't mean it will work again, and relying on an existing heuristic can make it difficult to see alternative solutions or come up with new ideas. Heuristics can lead to inaccurate judgments about how common things occur and how representative certain things may be.

In order to free ourselves from the lies, Great and Personal, that are inherent in all these difficult words and concepts, we must train ourselves and practice the skills of an Objective Observer. We must learn to gather objective data and challenge the absolutes and heuristics we've been told and taught. We must learn to look and think objectively and critically, without relying on shortcuts, assumptions, prejudices, or interpretations.

We've all heard the proverbial phrase "Is the glass half full or half empty?" Generally, this common expression is used to indicate that a particular situation could be a cause for pessimism (half empty) or optimism (half full), or as a general litmus test to simply determine an individual's worldview. The purpose of the question is to demonstrate that the situation may be seen in different ways depending on one's point of view and that there may be opportunity in the situation as well as trouble.

However, at its most basic level, the glass is neither half full nor half empty. The glass is simply a vessel with an amount of liquid in it. This is the data with which we're presented. This is the view of the Objective Observer; and as an Objective Observer, we can use this data to shape our working theory of optimism or pessimism, rather than twisting the data to fit.

Often I'll say to my therapy clients, "I have an eight-ounce vessel with four ounces of liquid in it. What is it?"

And often they will reply, "I know. I'm supposed to say it's half-full." My response to them is always the same: "No." To this, they will say, "Half-empty?" Again, I'll say, "No." It's simply an eight-ounce vessel with four ounces of liquid in it—data without prejudice, assumption, or interpretation that can become part of the ultimate choices they make in developing their own working theory.

An Objective Observer is also careful to distinguish opinions from facts. This is a critical step that can be really hard for most of us, because our opinions can *feel* like a fact. However, facts are *not* opinions, and opinions are *not* facts. We all know this, but it can be hard to tell the difference sometimes, especially when it comes to the lies, Great and Personal. Do you know the difference between fact and opinion?

Look at the list of statements below, and decide whether they are fact or opinion:

- I'm a bad person.
- My boss told me she didn't like my proposal.
- Nothing ever goes right.
- I'm not as attractive as they are.
- I failed the test.
- I'm overweight.
- I'm selfish.
- There is something wrong with me.
- I didn't give my son money when he asked for it.
- I don't deserve love. No one will ever love me.

THE OBJECTIVE OBSERVER

How did you do? Were you able to tell the facts from the opinions? Were you surprised to realize that six out of the ten statements were opinions, not facts? Compare your answers to the answers below:

- I'm a bad person. **Opinion**
- My boss told me she didn't like my proposal. **Fact**
- Nothing ever goes right. **Opinion**
- I'm not as attractive as they are. **Opinion**
- I failed the test. **Fact**
- I'm overweight. **Fact**
- I'm selfish. **Opinion**
- There is something wrong with me. **Opinion**
- I didn't give my son money when he asked for it. **Fact**
- I don't deserve love. No one will ever love me. **Opinion**

Facts and opinions are often uttered in the same breath, yet the terms have huge differences in their meanings. Whether a statement is a fact or an opinion depends on the validity of the statement. A fact refers to something that is true or real; is backed by evidence, documentation, etc.; and can be verified by anyone. On the other hand, an opinion is what a person believes or thinks about something. In finer terms, a fact is a proven entity, whereas opinion is a personal view that represents an individual's outlook and may or may not be based on facts or truth.

	FACT	**OPINION**
DEFINITION	Can be verified/ proven by anyone	A judgment or belief about something
BASED ON	Observation or research	Assumption or personal view
WHAT IS IT?	Objective reality	Subjective statement
VERIFICATION	Possible	Not possible
WORDS	Expressed with unbiased words	Expressed with biased words

Hopefully, it's clear by now that Objective Observers work hard to see and hear what is really there without bias or interpretation, not what they wish to or believe they should see and hear. They are gathering data before developing a working theory so that they can identify and free themselves from the lies, Great and Personal, and continue on the Hero's Journey to authentic selfhood and the lives they have always dreamed of.

But after becoming Objective Observers and developing this invaluable skill, how do we apply this ability to take the next step into the unknown and face the tests and challenges, the ordeal that's necessary to continue on the Hero's Journey?

We begin by identifying and challenging the lies.

CHAPTER XI

IDENTIFYING THE LIES

With truth you're able to grow and build upon it. Anything built on lies will eventually crumble and fall.
— **VARSHA SHARMA**

Remember the Great and Personal Lies that were covered in chapters II through VI? Or automatic thoughts, that stream of negative thinking that seems to pop into our minds automatically? And what about negative ideas about ourselves, the world, and our future?

Identifying and challenging the lies, Great and Personal, that live in our automatic negative thoughts is where all these ideas come together.

On the Hero's Journey, when crossing the threshold from the known into the unknown, we must use all our skills as Objective Observers to be aware of the link between what happens in the world around us, the thoughts and feelings that arise in response to those happenings, and the behaviors and actions we choose as a result. Fortunately, we all have a built-in early warning system to alert us to the lies, Great and Personal, that are beginning to enslave and have their way with us.

Something happens in the world around us; and before we know it, an uncomfortable feeling we don't like comes over us. Some of us may notice that feeling in our heads because of that negative voice that's always judging us, making us feel stupid, unworthy, unlovable, dizzy, or light-headed. Others may notice that feeling in their mouth, which is suddenly dry, and feel unable to speak. Still others may notice that feeling in their throat or chest, as if they can't swallow or breathe comfortably and naturally or their heart is beating unusually fast. We may also notice that feeling in our arms or legs, as though we're suddenly unable to move or hold ourselves upright. Or we may notice that feeling in the pit of the stomach, as if it's uncomfortably tight or rolling around with upset.

That feeling that something is wrong, no matter where we may notice it in our minds and/or bodies, is created by the lies, Great and Personal, that rob us of ourselves and our choices, forcing us to do, say, and be things that cause us to live in misery. Those lies literally chain our minds and bodies, robbing us of the will to challenge, fight back, and break the chains of misery that automatic negative thoughts are made from.

Something happens in the world around us, and that uncomfortable feeling we don't want to feel can actually become our greatest ally in the tests, challenges, and ordeal of the Hero's Journey. That uncomfortable feeling that most of us would like to avoid or turn away from is our early warning sign that the thoughts we have that are built on lies, Great and Personal, are at work. It's our signal that it's time to become Objective Observers, identify what has happened, see it as data without prejudice or interpretation, and examine and challenge the automatic negative thoughts—the lies—that are inherent in our thinking.

Megan's story may be hard to read because of her

IDENTIFYING THE LIES

history of generational abuse. Unfortunately, it's an all-too-common story. Megan grew up in a very close and private family, with a grandfather and a father who were unable—or unwilling—to control their anger. When the men became angry, they took their anger out on their wives. Megan was terrified every time her father got mad, because she knew it meant that her mother was in danger; and her stomach would rebel even though her mother told her over and over that everything was okay and that her father loved her very much.

As Megan grew older, her stomach tried to tell her again and again that something was wrong every time someone in her life became angry. Not surprisingly, toward the end of high school, when Megan fell in love with a boy who had difficulty controlling his anger, she started having stomach pains that were severe enough to send her to the emergency room more than once. Throughout her late teens and early twenties, she saw doctor after doctor, had test after test, and tried to figure out what was wrong with her. Finally, one of her doctors suggested she might want to "talk to someone" about how to live with constant stomach pain.

By the time Megan came to see me, she had tried everything she could think of and was skeptical that "talking about pain so obviously in my body will be able to help anything." Nonetheless, she was feeling at her wit's end and desperate for relief. So we talked about her stomach pain, exploring many different aspects of her experience of it. When I asked about her earliest memory of this experience, Megan doubled over in severe pain. Looking at me with tears in her eyes, Megan told me, "I was six years old, I think, and my father was mad about something my mom did, and he was hitting her so hard that she was crying. We went to the ER with her that night. I felt sick the whole time."

Over the course of our time together, Megan connected an entire history of feeling sick every time someone important in her life got irritated or angry. Her stomach had been trying to tell her that something was wrong in a time when she was too young to understand and process in words, so her body "spoke" in the only way she could understand. Megan worked hard at "talking to somebody" to understand what her stomach was trying to tell her and to separate truth from lies when faced with other people's irritation or anger.

So how do we do all that?

Well, instead of avoiding, turning away from, or hiding from that uncomfortable feeling, we need to think back to what was happening around us in the moments before we started to feel uncomfortable. We need to write down what happened so it's there in front of us instead of skittering around in our mind, trying to get away. After that, we need to write down all the automatic negative thoughts that sprang up in our minds as a result of what happened. Not just the first one or the first few thoughts, but *all* of them, because automatic negative thoughts always travel in packs. One negative thought seems to turn naturally into another, and another, and another; and before long, there is a whole series of cascading negative thoughts leading to a terribly distressing end.

Perhaps your response to this is "Write it down? What do you mean *write it all down?*" or "But I hate writing things down. It's too hard. I won't have time. I don't like to write."

Over time I've heard countless variations on this theme

from people of all different ages, genders, races, shapes, and sizes. Writing appears to bring up all kinds of different things for different people. This is exactly what makes writing so valuable. It brings things up, makes them real, and helps us look at our thoughts and feelings directly and objectively, which allows us to deal with them in ways that just thinking about them or talking about them don't do.

In the 1980s, researcher James Pennebaker "accidentally discovered the power of writing" while studying writing via freewriting, a method used by creative writers for many years. Pennebaker contends that regular journaling strengthens immune cells known as T lymphocytes. He believes that writing about stressful events helps people come to terms with those events and acts as a stress management tool, thus reducing the impact of these stressors on one's physical health.

Since the 1980s, considerable research has been done on this type of writing, and a significant body of research has been built up in different areas. For example, expressive writing has been shown to help with the following:

- Improved lung function in asthma patients and reduced symptoms in rheumatism and arthritis patients

- Lowering resting blood pressure

- A reduction in physical symptoms and medical visits for cancer survivors

- Significantly greater reductions in anxiety and depressive symptoms as well as greater overall progress in psychotherapy

In addition to these more concrete benefits, regular therapeutic writing can help you find meaning in your experiences and view things from a new perspective. It can also lead to important insights about yourself and your environment that may be difficult to determine without focused writing. Scientific evidence supports that this kind of writing provides other unexpected benefits.

The act of writing accesses your left brain, which is analytical and rational. While your left brain is occupied, your right brain is free to create, intuit, and feel; and it affords the opportunity for unexpected solutions to seemingly unsolvable problems. Writing removes mental blocks created by the lies you've lived with and allows you to use all of your brainpower to better understand yourself, others, and the world around you.

Writing can clarify your thoughts, since taking a few minutes to jot down your thoughts and emotions (no editing!) will quickly get you in touch with your internal world. By writing routinely, you'll get to know what makes you feel happy and confident. You'll also become clear about situations and people who are toxic for you, which is important information for your emotional well-being. Writing about anger, sadness, and other painful emotions helps to release the intensity of these feelings. By doing so, you're likely to feel calmer and better able to stay in the present. Writing about misunderstandings rather than stewing over them will help you understand the other person's point of view—and maybe you'll come up with a sensible resolution to the conflict. And finally, writing allows you to track patterns, trends, improvement, and growth over time. When current circumstances appear insurmountable, you'll be able to look back on previous dilemmas that you've since resolved.

So how does this look in the real world? When Megan

IDENTIFYING THE LIES

began to write down what she had been thinking and telling herself when her stomach ached, she was able to see the link between her stomach pain and her experience and fear of other people's anger. The "something that happened" in Megan's life—whether it was her father yelling, a boyfriend getting angry, her boss talking to her in a curt tone, or her best friend sharing her frustration over Megan always feeling bad—triggered thoughts that the other person's anger, irritation, or frustration was dangerous. Her thoughts of this danger led to her anticipation of a violent outburst from those people despite the fact that, with the exception of her father, Megan hadn't experienced violent reactions as a result of other people's difficult feelings. And with that anticipation of a violent outburst, Megan's stomach would begin to hurt.

Like any new skill or ability you want to develop, identifying what happened and writing out your thoughts will take practice and some getting used to. You need to pay active attention to the thoughts (i.e., lies) in your head rather than assuming that what you're thinking is right, normal, natural, or what everybody thinks. You need to become the Objective Observer, the Sherlock Holmes of your own experience. You need to stop those lies in their tracks, pin them down, and examine them instead of letting them spin out of control the way they always have. You need to learn to recognize and control the lies rather than letting the lies control you.

The first few times you try to pay attention to your thoughts and write them down will likely feel clunky, unnatural, and very uncomfortable, just like how the first few times you got on a bicycle felt the same way. But just like learning to ride a bike, you need to keep trying and keep writing until the act of writing those automatic negative thoughts comes more easily and naturally and becomes more familiar, if not more comfortable.

You may also notice that what makes writing those automatic negative thoughts down a challenge is that writing something down puts it in black and white right in front of us, making it harder to look away and avoid or ignore them. You may wince and find yourself thinking, "Is that really what's in my head? Is that really what I say about myself? Is that really the story I tell myself?" Writing down the negative, punishing, self-defeating, sometimes hateful words (i.e., lies) that echo in our minds and torture us often makes real the extent to which we're slaves to the ideas, beliefs, and values (lies) that are hurtful, limiting, and enslaving. For Megan, this part of her journey was quite painful; recalling incidents where she was faced with the anger, irritation, or frustration of others began with fear based on early childhood experience and ended with the current experience of stomach pain.

For many on the Hero's Journey, this is where the first of the tests and challenges will emerge. Having crossed the threshold into the unknown, we must learn new ways of looking, thinking, feeling, and being. Embracing that uncomfortable feeling as our early warning sign, being an Objective Observer to identify what happened, and using writing to identify the lies and automatic negative thoughts become the weapons that give us a fighting chance in the battle to become the Hero of our own lives.

So practice, practice, practice. Hone your skills. Build and strengthen your weapons. Face the tests and challenges head-on, because you're on the path to freedom

IDENTIFYING THE LIES

and selfhood; and there is no other way to become a Hero than to go forward.

Every day, maybe multiple times a day, take paper and pen and think back over your day to the moment(s) when that familiar, uncomfortable feeling raised its head inside you. Got it? Good. Now think back even further to find the "something that happened" that came before the uncomfortable feeling. Chances are you won't have to think back very far—maybe a minute or two, or even less. Perhaps you were doing something, and it wasn't going well or as you had hoped. Maybe you were talking with someone, and something you said or they said led to the uncomfortable feeling. Or maybe you were sitting alone, thinking about something or someone, and that feeling washed over you. Whatever it may be, write down what happened, not your interpretations or feelings about it. Write it as simply and completely as possible, without judgment or prejudice. Be an Objective Observer as you write it down. Be Sergeant Joe Friday, and write down, "Just the facts, ma'am." Be Sherlock Holmes and write down only the facts of "something that happened."

Got it? Great!

Next, put yourself back in that "something that happened" and all the thoughts that came into your head before the uncomfortable feeling arrived. Write down the cascade of automatic negative thoughts, from the first one to the last, one after another, until you get to the end. Write, write, write. Even if what you're writing doesn't seem to make a lot of sense, keep writing those automatic negative thoughts until you come to the end. You'll know you're there when that uncomfortable feeling finds its way back into you. You'll know because that uncomfortable feeling is so familiar, and you'll want to run away from it, avoid it, and stop thinking about whatever started it.

At this point, it's important to recognize that this, the beginning of the tests and challenges, is hard work. You're purposely remembering in order to bring back that uncomfortable feeling; and for as long as you can remember, you've worked hard to run away from and avoid anything and everything that brings that uncomfortable feeling. But you need that uncomfortable feeling, because it's going to be your greatest ally in your battle against the lies, Great and Personal, that have chained and enslaved you all your life.

This is hard work, because you'll have to write down the automatic negative thoughts—those lies, Great and Personal Lies, that have tortured you for as long as you can remember. You have to face the monster standing in your path on your Hero's Journey and use the skills you've developed and the weapons you've honed to defeat it. And doing battle with the monsters in our head takes strength, willpower, and courage. The same courage that helped you to survive all the years of misery and distress can now be harnessed to fight the battle and set you free.

Face the monster. Write down the "something that happened" and the whole cascade of lies and automatic negative thoughts. Then take the next step on the Hero's Journey by examining the evidence, challenging the lies, and slaying the monster—that uncomfortable feeling that the lies created and have kept painfully alive as long as you can remember—and live the life you've dreamed of.

CHAPTER XII

EXAMINING THE EVIDENCE AND CHALLENGING THE LIES

Everything we hear is an opinion, not a fact.
Everything we see is a perspective, not the truth.
— **MARCUS AURELIUS**

Examining the evidence and challenging the lies begins by recognizing the lies. This will require you to compare what you've just written down to the list of automatic negative thoughts and the Great and Personal Lies.

"Okay, that doesn't sound too hard," you may be saying. "I should be able to recognize a lie when I see one."

That may be true, but be careful. This is where your skills as an Objective Observer need to be strictly applied, because these lies have been in your head so long that they may seem like truth to you, disguising themselves as "things that everybody knows." This is where it's critical to separate the facts (which can be observed and verified by anyone and expressed in nonbiased words) from opinion (which are judgments or beliefs based on assumptions or personal views and are expressed in biased language). This is where it's vital that you allow yourself to explore *all* the possibilities, not just the ones you've always known or that come conveniently into your head.

Let's use an example of a cascade of thoughts that has likely happened to you before:

- First thought: "My boss didn't say hello and smile at me this morning."
- Next thought: "She looked angry."
- Next thought: "I'm in trouble."
- Next thought: "She hates me."
- Next thought: "I'm going to get fired."
- Next thought: "I can't do anything right."
- Next thought: "I'm a total failure."

Sound familiar? For many people, some version of this scenario has unfortunately played through their heads in a seemingly endless loop of anxious and negative thoughts—an endless loop of lies.

Let's be an Objective Observer, take the thoughts one at a time, and evaluate which ones are facts and which ones are opinions.

- First thought: "My boss didn't say hello and smile at me this morning." **Fact**—this "something that happened" can be observed and verified by anyone and expressed in nonbiased language.
- Next thought: "She looked angry." **Opinion**—this isn't "something that happened," but rather a judgment or belief based on an assumption or personal view and expressed in biased language.
- Next thought: "I'm in trouble." **Opinion**—again, this is a judgment or belief based on an assumption or personal view and expressed in biased language.
- Next thought: "She hates me." **Opinion**—this is

EXAMINING THE EVIDENCE AND CHALLENGING THE LIES

another judgment or belief based on an assumption or personal view and expressed in biased language.

- Next thought: "I'm going to get fired." **Opinion**—this is yet another judgment or belief based on an assumption or personal view and expressed in biased language.

- Next thought: "I can't do anything right." **Opinion**—this is also a judgment or belief based on an assumption or personal view and expressed in biased language.

- Next thought: "I'm a total failure. I'll never succeed. I'll never be happy." **Opinion**—this final thought is also a judgment or belief based on an assumption or personal view and expressed in biased language.

You may have noticed how one fact—the "something that happened"—led to a whole overwhelming cascade of anxious, negative opinions. This is your first piece of evidence that these thoughts are based on and biased by lies. Now your job is to figure out which of the lies, Great and Personal, are at work.

In figuring out which of these lies, Great and Personal, are at work in your thoughts, it can be helpful to have the list in front of you to remind you of their existence.

THE GREAT LIES

- Happily Ever After: You should feel happy all the time about everything.

- I Can't: You believe and/or embrace the limits imposed on you.

- Never, Always, Perfect: You believe in unattainable ideals.
- No Choice: You trap yourself in an impossible corner and give up responsibility.

THE PERSONAL LIES

- All-or-Nothing Thinking: You engage in black-and-white thinking.
- Overgeneralization: You have generalized a single instance into an overall pattern.
- Mental Filter: You focus on a single negative and exclude all of the positives.
- Disqualifying the Positives: You acknowledge but reject any positives.
- Jumping to Conclusions—Mind Reading: You believe you know what others are thinking.
- Jumping to Conclusions—Fortune-Telling: You believe you can predict the future.
- Magnification or Minimization: You exaggerate or minimize the importance of things.
- Emotional Reasoning: You engage in thoughts such as *I feel this way, so it must be true.*
- "Should" Statements: You engage in thoughts that are usually based on other's expectations and that begin with phrases such as *I should, I ought to,* or *I must.*

EXAMINING THE EVIDENCE AND CHALLENGING THE LIES

- Labeling/Mislabeling: You assign value or judgment on the basis of one instance.

- Personalization: You take everything personally.

- Control Fallacy: You have no control or complete control.

- Fallacy of Fairness: You assume that life is fair.

- Fallacy of Change: You expect or pressure others to change so they can meet your needs.

- Always Being Right: You must always be right, correct, or accurate.

- Heaven's Reward Fallacy: You believe that suffering and hard work will be result in a just reward.

Let's test those opinions from the earlier example that began with the factual statement, "My boss didn't say hello and smile at me this morning."

"SHE LOOKED ANGRY"

This opinion/thought has a number of lies in it, the first of which is #5, Jumping to Conclusions—Mind Reading. Your boss didn't say hello and smile, and you decided that she wasn't smiling because she was angry. But we all know there are lots of reasons why people don't smile. Sometimes they don't smile because they are angry. Other times, they don't smile because they may be unhappy, distracted, worried, in a hurry, or feeling unwell. So when we decide someone doesn't smile at us because they are angry, we assume—or jump to a conclusion—that we can read their mind and know that they are angry. We've fallen victim to a lie.

The second lie in this opinion/thought that "She looked angry" is #3, Mental Filter. Your boss didn't smile, and you focused on this single negative assumption—this judgment of her mood—and discarded all the positives. You ignored or forgot about all the times she did smile as well as the expression on her face whenever she told you she was angry. You ignored or forgot all the other reasons that people sometimes have certain expressions on their faces. You filtered out all the countless expressions you've seen on your boss's face and all the positives in your experience with your boss so that the lie could have its way with you and lead you to believe that she was angry.

The third lie that applies here is #7, Magnification or Minimization, where you exaggerate or minimize the importance of things. Your boss didn't say hello and smile; and for you, this became the single most important indicator of how your boss was feeling. This one morning of not saying hello and smiling convinced you that the only reason your boss didn't do these things is that she was angry.

Finally, the fourth lie that applies is #10, Labeling/Mislabeling, where you assign value or judgment on the basis of one instance using highly emotional or loaded language. Your boss didn't say hello and smile at you this morning; and the lie told you a judgment, which led to a highly emotional, negatively loaded thought.

By examining the lies in this first negative automatic thought, it should be clear that when we allow ourselves to believe that automatic negative thoughts are truth, we're actually allowing ourselves to be misled and enslaved by lies. We're allowing our thinking to be biased and twisted into a misery of our own making—a misery that need not be.

Let's keep following the stream of automatic negative thoughts and see how many more lies are creating our misery.

"I'M IN TROUBLE"

This opinion/thought also contains a number of lies. You may have recognized #3, Mental Filter, and #7, Magnification or Minimization. Did you also identify #6, Jumping to Conclusions—Fortune Telling? When an automatic negative thought convinces you that you know the future and can predict what is going to happen, you become caught in another lie.

"SHE HATES ME"

The lies in this opinion/thought should look familiar. The lie of Mind Reading has trapped your thoughts again and joined forces with Mental Filter, Magnification/Minimization, and Personalization to strengthen your misery, wrapping you in a web of negative thoughts that enslave you to misery.

"I'M GOING TO GET FIRED"

As the web of lies and misery grows and tightens around you, Mental Filter, Magnification/Minimization, and Personalization again join forces with Fortune Telling to drag you further into distress.

"I CAN'T DO ANYTHING RIGHT"

As the number and misery of the Personal Lies grow longer and deeper—Mental Filter, Magnification/Minimization, Mind Reading, Fortune Telling, Personalization, Labeling/Mislabeling—often the Great Lies join in. This opinion/thought has latched onto the Great Lie of *I Can't*.

"I'M A TOTAL FAILURE. I'LL NEVER SUCCEED. I'LL NEVER BE HAPPY"

The cascade of opinion/thoughts invariably ends with a final, often all-encompassing negative judgment of yourself and your future. It traps you, enslaving you to a future of misery fueled by the Great Lies absolutes of *total* and *never* and guaranteeing that Happily Ever After is forever out of reach.

In all, a single instance of "something that happened" triggered a cascade of automatic negative thoughts (i.e., opinions) that seem and feel true—and, as you come to believe, must be true—because they are the unexamined, unchallenged Great and Personal Lies that have been the cause of your misery for as long as you can remember. These are the lies that have kept you from becoming the Hero of your own life. And these unexamined, unchallenged lies are the tests and challenges you must face, the ordeal you must undergo to free yourself from the slavery of misery and hopelessness.

You can become an Objective Observer. You can learn to separate facts from opinions. You can identify the lies, Great and Personal, that have enslaved and tortured you. And then you can challenge those lies, triumph in the ordeal, and return as the Hero you were always meant to be.

EXAMINING THE EVIDENCE AND CHALLENGING THE LIES

Something That Happened: "My boss didn't say hello and smile at me this morning."

AUTOMATIC THOUGHT	CHALLENGE
"She looked angry." Types of lies: Mental Filter, Mind Reading, Magnification, Labeling/Mislabeling	My boss might not have seen me. My boss might be worried about something. My boss might be distracted. My boss might not be feeling well.
"I'm in trouble." Lies: Mental Filter, Mind Reading, Magnification, Personalization, Fortune Telling	I haven't done anything to get myself in trouble.
"She hates me." Lies: Mental Filter, Mind Reading, Magnification, Personalization	My boss and I have always gotten along pretty well.
"I'm going to get fired." Lies: Mental Filter, Magnification, Personalization, Fortune Telling	If my boss had a problem with me or my work, she would have told me.
"I can't do anything right." Lies: Mental Filter, Magnification, Personalization, I Can't	I do a lot of things right—and if I do something wrong, I can fix it.
"I'm a total failure. I'll never succeed. I'll never be happy." Lies: Mental Filter, Magnification, Personalization, Fortune Telling, Absolutes (Never, Always, Perfect)	I do a good job, and I can manage whatever comes along.

Did you notice that the words in the Challenges column were dealing with the situation without distortions, assumptions, judgments, or prejudice? Or that they avoided negative "working theories" and were stated in ways that were objective and expressed in unbiased words? Did you also notice that none of the challenges used words or ideas that were self-hating, hurtful, limiting, or enslaving? Or that, as you worked through the challenges, uncomfortable feelings didn't have a chance to build a web of misery inside you?

You may also have noticed that, like with learning to write down all your automatic negative thoughts, it may feel clunky and unnatural the first few times you try to challenge the lies. It may be hard to come up with a challenge that's stated without distortions, assumptions, judgments, or prejudice and in objective, unbiased words. And just like learning to write down all your automatic negative thoughts, you'll need to practice, practice, practice to come up with the challenges that overwhelm the lies, Great and Personal, and triumph in the ordeal that's necessary to become the Hero of your own life.

In order to challenge the lies, Great and Personal, you'll need to use your skills as an Objective Observer, be a Fair Witness, and report only what you directly experience or witness. You'll need to access your analytical and rational left brain, which (with practice) can recognize the distortions, assumptions, and judgments; as well as your creative, intuitive right brain to find new solutions and possibilities for seemingly unsolvable problems. You'll need to allow yourself to suspend disbelief and imagine possibilities you've never considered before.

And just as the power of writing can reveal and make real the negative, punishing, self-defeating words—the lies—that echo in our minds and torture us, the power

EXAMINING THE EVIDENCE AND CHALLENGING THE LIES

of writing can also help with making the challenges real. Because, as you may remember, writing something down puts it down in black and white right in front of us, making it harder to avoid or ignore it. Writing out the challenges accesses your left brain while affording your right brain the opportunity it needs. It removes mental blocks created by the lies, Great and Personal, you've lived with and frees you to use all your brainpower to break the chains (i.e., lies) that have bound and enslaved you. Writing the challenges can make them your sword and shield in the battle to be the Hero of your own life.

So challenge the lies. Challenge. Challenge.

Every day. Maybe even multiple times a day.

Hone your skills. Build and strengthen your sword and shield. Triumph in the ordeal, and win the reward that has been waiting for you—the reward of your own truth—so that you can cross the threshold once more and be resurrected, reborn as the Hero of your own life.

Again, this is hard work, and the lies will likely try to return once more to enslave you. The lies, Great and Personal, have had control of you, have had their way with you to create distress and misery for many, many years. They won't give up easily. They will try to grab you again when you're feeling vulnerable, tired, defeated, or weak. And when you feel this way, the lies, Great and Personal, will try to take advantage of it.

This is when you'll once again need to become an Objective Observer. To write down the "something that happened" and the cascade of automatic negative thoughts. To separate fact from opinion. You'll need to examine the evidence and identify the Great and Personal Lies—and then challenge the lies to take back your own truth.

You must do this again, and again, and again. And before long, your skills will rise up more easily and come to you more naturally, and you'll triumph in the ordeal and continue on your path as the Hero of your own life.

Remember Megan from chapter XI? The young woman whose stomach pains had bothered her for years as the result of childhood experiences that taught her to believe that other people's anger, irritation, or frustration led to violent outbursts? The first few times she wrote out her automatic negative thoughts, it was a real challenge for her to separate fact from opinion and then to recognize the lies, Great and Personal, in those thoughts. But as she practiced being an Objective Observer again and again, her ability to look and remember without personal bias or assumption got easier and easier. What surprised Megan most was that, once she became accustomed to looking at the automatic negative thoughts—the lies—in this way, it also became much easier to challenge them. The possibilities for what was going on around her beyond what the lies "told" her freed her thoughts and feelings; and as she allowed herself to consider more possibilities, her stomachaches occurred less and less frequently. Now, when her stomach aches, Megan knows that something in her thinking may be inaccurate and reacting to lies, and she is able to calm her thoughts as well as her internal reactions and choice.

You must also know that when you triumph over the lies, Great and Personal, when the truth is revealed, sometimes anger follows. It may be anger at yourself for believing the lies; anger at others for telling you that the lies, Great and Personal, were truth. Anger at all the distress, misery, and suffering you've endured; or anger at being enslaved for

EXAMINING THE EVIDENCE AND CHALLENGING THE LIES

years and years. Anger may bubble up after years of being pushed down because anger is a complex and difficult response for many of us. It's one of those uncomfortable emotions we would rather avoid than face or deal with.

Everybody feels anger at different times and to varying degrees. It's simply part of the human experience. Feelings of anger can arise in many different contexts. Experiencing unjust treatment, hearing a criticism, or simply not getting what you want are but a few of the potential triggers. The experience of anger can range from mild irritation to frustration, all the way up to seething rage. Even boredom is a mild version of anger in the form of dissatisfaction with what is happening.

However, there are times when other emotions may spur the anger, and we use anger to protect the raw feelings that lie beneath it. Learning to recognize anger as not only a basic and valid emotion, but also as a protector of those raw feelings, can be incredibly powerful.

Why is anger good sometimes? Without feelings of anger, we wouldn't take a stand against unfairness or injustice. Anger is an internal alarm that tells us something isn't quite right. Anger can tell us when a lie, Great or Personal, is trying to sneak back in and enslave us again.

On the following page is what the Gottman Institute calls the Anger Iceberg, because it shows other emotions and feelings that may be lurking below the surface. It shows the kinds of thoughts and feelings that the lies, Great and Personal, can trigger and that try to enslave and control us if we let them, even after we've finished our Hero's Journey.

Early in my career as a psychologist, I worked with Scott. He had faced and conquered many lies, Great and

What you show / what others see

Anger

What you think / feel

Trauma   Stress   Insecurity
Disappointment   Guilt
Rejection
Anxiety   Shame
Embarassment
Depression
Hurt   Fear

Personal, and was ready to begin his own path back to reward, resurrection, and return. Scott had become an excellent Objective Observer, ready to feel and accept the full range of emotions, good and not so good, without getting stuck anywhere. I had warned Scott that anger around his former way of thinking, feeling, and being might follow; and he felt confident that he would recognize any feelings that emerged and could manage them.

Several weeks later, Scott described a fairly minor incident at a stop light that made him aware of his years of unexpressed anger. Scott was waiting for the green arrow to allow him to turn left while cars going straight ahead were moving past while the driver behind him was honking their horn continuously. That honking felt like a continuous reminder that Scott was doing something wrong—that he wasn't accommodating others as he had

EXAMINING THE EVIDENCE AND CHALLENGING THE LIES

always been taught to do, even when that made things more difficult for him. Scott felt caught in the old way he knew so well.

And then he felt angry.

Scott turned off his car, walked back to the car behind him, and proceeded to "tell off" the driver in the car behind him. Although Scott was surprised by his own reaction and response, he was able to make a different, more self-affirming, Heroic choice.

Scott's anger told him that "something was wrong." He knew that he was doing the safe and right thing, but the lie being told loudly by the driver behind him was trying to push him back into accepting lies and accommodating others even when he knew that would only lead his to distress. Scott's angry reaction, which he was now able to recognize and connect to a lie, was an internal alarm, alerting him and preparing him to challenge the lie and make thinking and behavior choices he felt good about.

So the next time you feel anger in any of its forms, spend some time being an Objective Observer and use the Anger Iceberg to help you identify the feelings giving rise to the anger. Once you know what the feelings underneath the surface are, you can analyze them to figure out what your internal alarm is telling you. You can figure out whether this anger is a normal response to injustice and unfairness, or whether it's part of a lie, Great or Personal, that's trying to enslave you again and drag you away from your Hero's Journey.

Keep fighting those lies, Great and Personal, and walking your own path to remain the Hero of your own life. In the words of Winston Churchill, "[T]his is the lesson: never give in, never give in, never, never, never, never—in nothing, great or small, large or petty—never give in except to convictions of honor and good sense."

CHAPTER XIII

OVERCOMING THE OBSTACLES:
ANXIETY, DEPRESSION, AND TRAUMA

*Say not, "I have found the truth," but
rather, "I have found a truth."*
— **KAHLIL GIBRAN**

Anxiety, depression, and the aftereffects of trauma are often the most difficult and unpleasant emotions that many of us face in our lives. As discussed earlier, anxiety and depression are normal reactions to difficult interactions and situations and have evolved over time to help individuals survive better and learn to thrive in a challenging environment. Trauma is one of those difficult interactions or situations that individuals survive and often results in anxiety and depression. All three of these distressing emotions have something important in common: they are usually triggered by a lack of control and our desire to regain control.

When we feel anxious, that anxiety is often connected to our inability to control the things or people or situations around us. In a similar fashion, when we become depressed, it's often connected to our lack of control over the ways in which others perceive, treat, or interact with us. Trauma is connected to the lack of control over what happens to us in terrible situations as well as our desire to never find ourselves with such a lack of control in the future.

But the reality of control is that it's not real—it's an illusion. The illusion of control is the devil in service to the lies, Great and Personal, that enslave and torture us throughout our lives. None of us have control over when we're born or when we die, and most of us have (grudgingly) accepted these realities. What is harder for most of us is that we also have no control over much of what happens to us in our lives and absolutely *no* control over how others react to, treat, perceive, speak to, or interact with us. We have no control over other people in our lives and our world.

And yet our thoughts and beliefs, which are the lies, Great and Personal, tell us that we do have control. If we could be different, do something different, or say something different, we could control how others perceive, react to, treat, speak to, and interact with us. The devilish lie of control tells us that if only we could give others what they want, need, or demand from us, we could relax and be happy in the ways we've imagined. We allow the lie of control, especially control over others and our world, to control us, our reactions, our thoughts, and our choices. We don't question whether our reactions, thoughts, and choices will contribute to our own well-being and happiness because we believe that if we're different, we'll have control over how others perceive, react to, treat, speak to, and interact with us. We've embraced the illusion of control over others; and this leads to the anxiety, depression, and aftereffects of trauma that many suffer.

Some of the most difficult thoughts—the lies—that plague many of the people I work with go something like this:

- "If only I could get my father to listen to me, then I

wouldn't have to make so many mistakes and I could be more successful."

- "If only I could get my wife to say no to the kids, then I wouldn't have to yell at them so much."
- "If only I could find a job where I didn't have an idiot for a boss, then I could finally get my career to take off."
- "If only I could get my husband to stop drinking so much, then we could have a good life together."
- "If only my daughter would break it off with that woman she's been living with, then we could get back to having a normal family and I wouldn't have to lie about her."
- "If only my son would get a job, then we wouldn't have to give up our retirement to take care of him."

If only, if only, if only. What all these people were saying in one way or another was that if only the world around them would change—if only other people would change—then they could be happy, successful, less anxious, or less afraid. If only other people and situations would change to accommodate their needs and wishes, then everything would be perfect. All these people are saying that if only they had the power to control and change others—and there it is again, the lie of control. So, I'll repeat this important truth. We have absolutely no control over how others react to, treat, perceive, speak to, or interact with us. We have no control over other people in our lives and our world.

So if control is an illusion—a lie—is there anything we can do? Is there anything we can control?

Yes! And yes!

There is one critically important thing you can control; one thing that can make the difference between enslavement to lies and misery and becoming the Hero of your own life. One thing that can change a life filled with anxiety, depression, and the aftereffects of trauma to one filled with your own definitions of joy. That thing is you.

You have to recognize and live the reality that the only thing, the only person, over which you have control is you. You have to choose and challenge your thoughts. You have to choose how you react to the things that happen and the reactions of others. You have to challenge the lies, Great and Personal, that come up when something happens. You have to choose how you'll react and respond. You have to choose to react and respond in a way that reflects who you are. You have to choose to act and react out of your own values and beliefs. You have to act out of your own truth. You have to choose to act as the Hero of your own life.

Others may choose to respond to us in a way that's thoughtless, unkind, or even mean; and we can't control that. But we can choose not to allow others to treat us badly, not to accept their thoughtless, unkind, or mean reactions, responses, and interactions. We can choose not to allow their thoughts, beliefs, and judgments about us—and their actions toward us—to become the lies, Great and Personal, that we believe and make a part of us. We can choose to examine the thoughts that come up when something happens. We can use our skills and abilities as Objective Observers to analyze them and choose what to think about them. And we can use our hard-won

OVERCOMING THE OBSTACLES

knowledge of our own truth to choose how to respond to them. We can choose to act as the Hero of our own life.

I know how hard it can be to find space in your head to stop the lies, Great and Personal, to challenge them and choose your own truth when the lies have been there for so long. When the lies leap into action and spin in our heads, it can feel like they fill all the space, leaving no room for choosing and challenging. Knocking that negative train off the tracks when it's already full steam ahead toward the misery that has been so familiar for so long may feel impossible. So you may want some help in making room in your head for choosing and challenging. Luckily, there are lots of ways to do this that have a strong basis in science and what we know about how our brains, thoughts, and emotions work.

In the exhibits at the back of this book, you'll find a list and descriptions of forty-two different techniques for coping with anxious and depressed feelings and the thoughts that may be taking up the space in your head that you need to challenge and choose. I encourage everyone I work with to try all the techniques over the course of about a month, because they work in different ways for different people. That being said, I also spend time explaining the first three techniques, in addition to humor and sleep, because those techniques are a little different from the rest. Those skills have the strongest basis in physiology. That's important because physiologically we're all mammals; and I know that, when used correctly and consistently, everyone will get some degree of relief from their symptoms of anxiety and depression.

The first seven of these forty-two techniques also have something else in common: they stimulate the release of endorphins, our own homemade heroin. Endorphins are chemical messengers in our bodies that, when released, can help relieve pain and reduce stress and may cause a euphoric feeling. Endorphins are naturally occurring opioid-like substances that bind to the same receptors in our brains that heroin and opioid painkillers do without the habit-forming, addictive problems we've heard so much about. In short, they can make you feel really good and help create the space in your head to challenge and choose. And you can get an endorphin release anytime, anywhere you need or want one.

So how do you learn to do this? That's where these techniques come in.

BREATHE

How many times has someone told you to take a deep breath when you were feeling stressed, anxious, overwhelmed, or overcome by negative thoughts or feelings? They were on the right track, because the right kind of breathing stimulates an endorphin release. The problem, though, is that most people don't know how to breathe the right way.

What does it mean to breathe the right way? We've been breathing all our lives, since the moment we were born. How can we not know how to breathe the right way? How hard is it to take a deep breath? You just breathe in and hold it, right?

Actually, no. The right kind of breathing is different.

When most people take a deep breath, they only fill up the top third of their lungs, expanding the top third of their chest. This can put more pressure on the heart,

OVERCOMING THE OBSTACLES

which makes the heart beat harder and faster and can make most people feel short of breath and more anxious and depressed than ever. Whew! This is why the initial response I get from people I've worked with when I first mention deep breathing is often, "Yeah, I tried that, and it doesn't really work for me."

But the kind of deep breathing I'm talking about is diaphragmatic breathing, the kind of breathing that athletes and opera singers use. You see, diaphragmatic breathing means you pull oxygen all the way down to the bottom of your lungs; and when it's done properly, the top third of your chest doesn't move at all. So when all that oxygen-rich blood hits your brain, you get an endorphin release. Have you heard about the "runner's high"? Well, diaphragmatic breathing and the resulting endorphin release are what make that happen. And you can learn diaphragmatic breathing and get that same high without running a 5K or singing an opera.

Just lie on your bed on your back, without any pillows under your head, and breathe. You may notice that the top third of your chest doesn't move at all. Instead, your belly is moving up and down gently as you pull oxygen all the way in down to the bottom of your lungs. That's deep, diaphragmatic breathing. Keep breathing, low and slow; and be aware of what it feels like in your body when you breathe this way. Keep breathing this way until you feel like you can do this without thinking about it. Once it feels natural to you, put one pillow under your head, and keep practicing diaphragmatic breathing with one pillow until that feels natural too. Keep adding pillows under your head and practicing diaphragmatic breathing until you can do this sitting up.

Congratulations! You've mastered diaphragmatic breathing.

Practice this breathing technique many times a day when you feel relaxed and comfortable. You want to develop muscle memory for this kind of breathing so that, when you're feeling stressed, anxious, or depressed, you can do diaphragmatic breathing without even thinking about it. That way, you can get an endorphin release whenever and wherever you need or want it.

EAT CHOCOLATE

The second technique doesn't require any practice, but you may need to do a little shopping, because the second skill is eating chocolate. Don't get just any chocolate, though. You need dark chocolate—really dark—at least 70 percent cacao—because it not only stimulates the release of endorphins, but also contains serotonin, which is a neurotransmitter that fights depression. Dark chocolate also calms our central nervous system, which is the physiological system that gets overactive when we're anxious, stressed, or depressed.

So go shopping and find some dark chocolate that you like. I know that most people aren't crazy about the taste of dark chocolate, but there are lots of choices nowadays with additional flavors. You can find dark chocolate with almonds, berry flavors, coffee, or chilies. Any will do, as long as they are at least 70 percent cacao. And you don't have to eat the whole bar to get the benefits. A 2" x 2" square will give you the relaxing endorphin release you're looking for. Keep that dark chocolate near you all the time: in your desk, in your handbag, in the car, or anywhere else where you might need or want to calm your central nervous system. And whenever something happens that triggers those bad feelings and negative thoughts, eat a square of dark chocolate to create the space in your head that you need to challenge and choose.

AROMATHERAPY

I love when I talk to the people I work with about aromatherapy, because they tend to look at me like I've suggested that they go see a psychic or hang crystals around their home. Their reaction changes, though, when I tell them that aromatherapy is used in many hospitals to help calm patients in places like the emergency room, pre-op, post-op, and obstetrics. Hospitals use aromatherapy because science has established that aromas and smells have a direct link through our central nervous system to the limbic system (the part of the brain that controls emotions) as well as our heart rate, blood pressure, breathing, memory, stress, and hormone balance. Aromatherapy is the quickest and most foolproof way to calm yourself and make space in your head to do the work you need to choose and challenge.

Studies suggest that the most effective aromas to help you do this are lavender, chamomile, citrus, sage, bergamot, and peppermint. And don't worry that you have to walk around smelling like one of these fragrances. The best way to get the calming, soothing effects of one of these scents is to find an essential oil roller in the fragrance you like best and carry it with you. When you need or want that relaxation and mind-clearing effect, open the roller bottle, hold it under your nose, and take a big breath. Within seconds, the signals generated by the aromatherapy scent will travel to your limbic system and give you the relief you want or need. Keep a roller bottle in your pocket, desk, handbag, or car—just like with your dark chocolate—so it's everywhere and anywhere you might need it.

HUMOR

You've probably heard that it takes more muscles to frown than it does to smile, and that laughter is the best medicine. But did you know there is good science behind these sayings? This is one of the universal mysteries, yet the evidence is overwhelming that laughter relaxes the whole body, boosts the immune system, decreases stress hormones, and increases immune cells and infection-fighting antibodies, thus improving your resistance to disease. It also triggers the release of endorphins, protects the heart, improves the function of blood vessels, and increases blood flow, which can help protect you against heart attacks and other cardiovascular problems. In addition, laughter is known to increase creativity; improve problem-solving; enhance memory; elevate mood and feelings of well-being; reduce depression, anxiety, and tension; and increase self-esteem and resilience, hope, optimism, energy, and vigor. Laughter can even improve your relationships with others by its ability to increase bonding with friends and family as well as friendliness and attractiveness to others, which is probably why it's also associated with happier marriages and close relationships.

Laughter works so well for us because it dissolves distressing emotions. You can't feel anxious, angry, or sad when you're laughing. Laughter helps you relax and recharge, enabling you to stay focused and accomplish more. It also shifts perspective. Humor allows you to see situations in a more realistic and less threatening light. A humorous perspective creates psychological distance, which can help you avoid feeling overwhelmed.

The best part is that you don't even have to feel like laughing to get the benefits of laughter. You just have to laugh out loud for at least ten seconds to get the benefits that you can't get from smiling or feeling happy—and you don't have to respond to anything funny.

But if there is nothing striking you as funny, how do you laugh out loud? You can make your body laugh, make a laughing face, and make laughing sounds—whenever you need to. We all can. We've all had the experience of the "fake laugh," when we needed to laugh in a situation but didn't really feel like it. Making your body laugh out loud is very much like that, except that the "fake laugh" often doesn't last as long as you need to get the benefits of laughing. You need to laugh out loud continuously for ten seconds to get the physiological, mental, and emotional benefits of laughter. Ten seconds may last longer than you think when you're making yourself laugh out loud, so I often recommend that people count down the seconds on their ten fingers.

So practice laughing out loud every day, at least once a day, for ten seconds. I also recommend you do this laughing practice in private—in your car, in the shower, with your door closed—so you don't feel self-conscious and others don't look at you like you've lost your marbles. And the next time something happens and you start to feel anxious, depressed, or overwhelmed, take a deep breath and make yourself laugh out loud for ten seconds. Those endorphins will give you the lift and space in your head you need to be able to challenge and choose. Don't be surprised when laughing once a day turns into a whole lot more—that's how good laughing out loud helps us feel.

SLEEP

The news is always full of stories about America's sleep deficit and the disquieting fact that we can't "catch up" on sleep. Apparently, once you lose out on a good night's sleep, there is no way to make up for that loss except to get better at consistent, healthy sleep.

It's always surprising to me that, after all the years of schooling I've completed and all the years of practice with people from every walk of life, one of the most consistent problems I address with individuals is sleep. It's hard to overstate how important sleep is to our physical, mental, and emotional health. In fact, after water and food, sleep is a necessary condition of life, because it affects every part and system in our body. And the benefits of consistent, healthy sleep may be more wide-ranging than you imagined. For example, studies have shown that people who get enough healthy sleep on a consistent basis get sick less often, stay at a healthy weight, have a lower risk for serious health problems such as diabetes and heart disease, experience reduced stress and improved mood, think more clearly, do better in school and at work, get along better with people, make good decisions, and avoid injuries. (Sleepy drivers cause thousands of car accidents every year.)

OVERCOMING THE OBSTACLES

So what is healthy, consistent sleep? And how can you get it?

It's pretty widely understood and accepted that from the time we're in our mid-twenties to the day we die, the average adult needs between six to nine hours of sleep in every twenty-four-hour day. It's also clear that none of us is born knowing how to fall asleep, since before birth we could sleep and wake whenever our body needed to. That's why we have to help infants learn to fall asleep, and we have regular routines and rituals that help infants learn this critical life skill. We help our children's minds and bodies learn about sleep with the rituals and routines we follow every night before putting them down to sleep.

We may give them a bath and put them in soft, warm pajamas. We may keep the lights low and our voices soft. We may rock them in a rocking chair, read them a story, or sing them a song. We spend around thirty minutes teaching their little minds and bodies that they need to wind down and prepare to sleep, and we do this consistently over a matter of days and weeks until they learn how to help themselves go to sleep. Once children learn how to go to sleep, they generally can do this for themselves unless something happens that disrupts their sleep in a significant enough way that they have to learn sleep all over again.

In adult life, things happen all the time that can disrupt your ability to fall asleep and stay asleep. Or maybe you never really learned to sleep well. Regardless of the disruptor, adults must retrain themselves to sleep just as infants and children learn to sleep. Through the use of routines and rituals that become a regular, consistent series of activities that calm and relax our minds and bodies for approximately thirty minutes before we want to be asleep, we can learn to enjoy the consistent, healthy sleep we need to be able to challenge and choose.

So how do you start on the road back to consistently healthy sleep?

First, let's establish some ground rules. Your bed is for two things, and two things only—sleep and sex. Your bed isn't the place to watch television, use your computer, or look at your smartphone. In fact, those activities should be avoided completely for thirty minutes before you want to be asleep. All of our modern electronic devices emit the same kind of shortwave light that actually wakes up your brain, making falling asleep more difficult. Your bed is also not the place to eat, read, finish up work, or do other things many people do in bed. Your mind and body need to learn to associate your bed with sleep, and all the other things many of us tend to do in bed get in the way of that association.

In that same vein, your bed is also not a place to lie awake and wait to—or try to—fall asleep. This leads to another ground rule: never lie awake in bed longer than fifteen minutes. When you lie awake in bed longer than that, your brain and body associate lying awake with being in bed, which violates the first ground rule. If you find that you're still not asleep fifteen minutes after you lie down even after completing your sleep ritual or routine, get out of bed and do something calming and soothing until you feel tired enough to go back to bed and sleep. As you retrain your body and brain, you may have a number of nights in which you're in and out of bed every fifteen minutes until the association with bed and sleep becomes more established.

OVERCOMING THE OBSTACLES

These relatively challenging first few nights may result in you feeling tired in the days that follow, which leads to the third ground rule: no napping. You may remember that earlier I mentioned how the average adult needs between six and nine hours of sleep in any twenty-four-hour period, and those six to nine hours mean the total amount of time asleep. This means that if you nap for an hour or two during the day, those are one to two hours you won't sleep in your bed. So if you faithfully follow the healthy sleep guidelines, within a few days to a week you'll have successfully retrained your body and brain to a healthy, consistent sleep routine that you need for good physical, mental, and emotional health.

I've talked several times about a ritual or routine to help prepare you for sleep. The content of that ritual or routine can be whatever activities help you. These activities can include a small, warm, non-caffeinated beverage; a piece of dark chocolate; a warm bath; soothing music; calming reading (no murder mysteries, spy novels, or horror stories); or something creative like working in an adult coloring book. Some things you shouldn't do as part of your routine include no strenuous exercise after 5:00 p.m., no heavy eating after 8:00 p.m., and no alcohol, anti-anxiety medications, or sleep medications, since continued use interferes with your body's healthy sleep pattern.

After completing your routine to get ready for sleep, get into bed, turn the clock away from you, and try one of the following:

- Deep breathing
- Prayer or meditation

- Progressive muscle relaxation
- Visualization
- Guided imagery

These additional skills can relax you even further as you move toward sleep. You can find detailed descriptions of all these techniques in the exhibits at the back of this book.

Once you begin to enjoy consistent, healthy sleep, you may be tempted to abandon or shortcut your rituals and routines—but don't do that. Give yourself the gift of that fifteen to thirty minutes every night to focus on taking care of your body, mind, and spirit as you walk the road as the Hero of your own life. It can be easy to forget or ignore the importance of this kind of self-care because we're too busy, someone else needs it more, or we'll get to it tomorrow. We put everybody and everything ahead of taking care of ourselves because it would be selfish to take care of ourselves first. Interestingly, this definition of selfish is another Personal Lie.

Selfishness, as defined by the Oxford English Dictionary, is to be "lacking consideration for others; concerned chiefly with one's own personal profit or pleasure." This definition, though, calls into question what it means to be lacking in consideration for others. Are we lacking consideration for others when we know and honor what we need in order to be the Hero of our own lives? Are we lacking consideration for others when we recognize that we can't help or take care of others if we're so depleted by the demands and lies of others that we have nothing to give? Or is it the ultimate act of selfishness to ignore ourselves to the point of becoming utterly useless to ourselves and others?

This is the basic premise of the oxygen mask instructions we hear every time we board an airplane. It's the part of the preflight safety talk that starts with "This is a seatbelt..." and usually ends with "In the event of a loss in cabin pressure, oxygen masks will drop from the panel above your head. Pull the oxygen mask toward you and place it over your nose and mouth. Be sure to put your own oxygen mask on first before you try to help anyone else." Why do they tell you to "Be sure to put on your own oxygen mask first before you try to help anyone else"? Because if you can't breathe, you can't effectively help anyone else. If you pass out from lack of oxygen because you don't have your own oxygen mask on, the people you want to help or are trying to help will likely pass out too.

By now, the analogy should be obvious. If you aren't taking appropriate care of yourself, you can't take appropriate care of others. So whether you're recognizing that it's more selfish to uselessly sacrifice yourself, choosing to use your preferred stress relief techniques, consistently getting the healthy sleep you need, or challenging and intervening against the lies that try to enslave you, you must commit to you and your own truth to become and live as the Hero of your own life.

CHAPTER XIV

COMMITTING TO BECOMING AND BEING A HERO

For me, becoming isn't about arriving somewhere or achieving a certain aim. I see it instead as forward motion, a means of evolving, a way to reach continuously toward a better self. The journey doesn't end.
— **MICHELLE OBAMA**

All the techniques we've been exploring—diaphragmatic breathing, dark chocolate, aromatherapy, laughing out loud, and restful, restorative sleep—need consistent use and practice. These are the new habits you need to develop in order to successfully identify, challenge, and replace the old thinking habits of believing the lies, Great and Personal, that have kept you chained to misery for as long as you can remember. Consistency and repetition are the keys to creating and cementing these new habits that will be vital to becoming and remaining the Hero of your own life.

"Okay, so how many times do I have to practice these techniques?" you may be asking. "And for how long? Wait! I know! Everybody says it takes twenty-one days to form a new habit! So just three weeks, right?"

Well, like everything else in life, it depends. The science of habit formation and brain change gives us some good information and guidelines for how this works, what to expect, and where the idea that it takes twenty-one days to form a new habit came from.

In the 1950s, plastic surgeon Maxwell Maltz noticed a strange pattern among his patients. When he would perform an operation—a nose job, for example—he found that it would take the patient about twenty-one days to get used to seeing their new face. This prompted Maltz to think about his own adjustment to changes, and concluded that it took him about twenty-one days to form a new habit. Maltz wrote about these experiences and said, "These and many other commonly observed phenomena tend to show that it requires a minimum of about 21 days for an old mental image to dissolve and a new one to jell."

In 1960, Maltz published that quote and his other thoughts on behavior change in the book *Psycho-Cybernetics*. In the decades that followed, Maltz's work influenced a great many self-help professionals, from Zig Ziglar to Brian Tracy and Tony Robbins. As more and more people latched onto this simple story—like a very long game of Telephone—people forgot that he said "a minimum of about twenty-one days" and shortened it to, "It takes twenty-one days to form a new habit."

But the problem is that Maltz was simply observing what was going on around him and wasn't making a statement of fact. Furthermore, he had made sure to say that this was the minimum amount of time needed to adapt to a new change. So what is the real answer? How long does it take to form a habit? How long does it take a break a bad habit? Is there any science to back this up? And what does all of this mean for you and me?

In 2009, Phillippa Lally, a health psychology researcher at University College London, published a study

COMMITTING TO BECOMING AND BEING A HERO

in the *European Journal of Social Psychology* that was designed to figure out how long it actually takes to form a habit. This study found that, on average, it takes more than two months before a new behavior becomes automatic—sixty-six days, to be exact. And how long it takes a new habit to form can vary widely depending on the behavior, the person, and the circumstances. In Lally's study, it took anywhere from eighteen to 254 days for people to form a new habit. In other words, if you want to set your expectations appropriately, the truth is that it will probably take you anywhere from two to eight months—not twenty-one days—to build a new behavior into your life.

Before you let this dishearten you, let's talk about three reasons this research is actually inspiring. First, habits are formed in an area of your brain called the basal ganglia. Here, the more often you perform an action or behave a certain way, the more it gets physically wired into your brain. Your brain forms neuronal connections based on what you do repeatedly—both good and bad—in your life. Every time you act in the same way, a specific neuronal pattern is stimulated and becomes strengthened in your brain.

Second, the problem with changing your brain to form a new good habit—or break an old bad habit—is that enthusiasm is common, but commitment is rare. Knowing what to do is often not an issue; *committing* to it is the problem. Many of us lack the proper structures to support the behavioral changes our life goals require. Commitment, consistency, and patience are the hardest skills we've all had to learn to use to be better and improve daily, because making meaningful and long-lasting changes in life depends on your ability to form and execute new goal-achieving activities consistently enough that they become habitual.

Learning to practice consistently doesn't have to be half as hard as we make it on ourselves. Remember, there is no reason to get down on yourself if you try something for a few weeks and it hasn't become a habit yet. It's supposed to take longer than that! So there is no need to judge yourself if you can't master a behavior in twenty-one days. Also, you don't have to be perfect. Making a mistake once or twice has no measurable impact on your long-term habits. This is why you should treat failure like a scientist, give yourself permission to make mistakes, and develop strategies for getting back on track quickly. Finally, embracing longer timelines can help us realize that habits are a process and not an event. All of the "twenty-one days" hype can make it really easy to think, *Oh, I'll just do this, and it'll be done.* But habits don't work that way. You have to embrace the process. You have to commit to the system.

Becoming 1 percent better every day is a simple, practical way to achieve big goals. One percent seems like a small amount. Yes, it's tiny. But it's easy and doable—and it's applicable in most things you want to do or accomplish. It feels less intimidating and is more manageable. It might feel less exciting than chasing a huge win, but its results will be stronger and more sustainable.

Last but not least, find an accountability partner. The Association for Training Development conducted a study on accountability and found that you have a 65 percent chance of completing a goal if you commit to someone. And if you have a specific accountability appointment or deadline with a person you've committed to, you'll increase your chance of success by up to 95 percent. Goals

COMMITTING TO BECOMING AND BEING A HERO

take time, hard work, perseverance, and commitment to achieve; and results often don't come as quickly as you hope. But everything changes when you leverage an accountability system. To be accountable, all you need is a clear goal and a willingness to let others help you achieve it.

I know a lot about accountability. I had been saying for years that I wanted to write a book about everything I had learned in my years as a therapist, including the lies, Great and Personal, that had kept the people I worked with in misery. I had been telling people *forever* about becoming the Hero of your own life. But it wasn't until I told my colleagues that I was writing a book—even though I had barely started and had written only twenty pages—and asked them to hold me accountable that the book you're reading was written. And it wasn't until I found a publisher and told them I was in the midst of the first rewrite that they set a deadline for that first rewrite, and the book developed into something that could be successfully published. It was accountability (sharing a clear goal with my colleagues) and a deadline that brought the book you're reading to life. So find an accountability partner, or partners, and commit.

It may sound obvious, but committing to yourself and your own truth, which is the essence of the Hero's Journey, can also be difficult to do without help. Remember the picture of the Hero's Journey from chapter VII? It shows how, during Act I, there is the possibility that we may be aided by a sage or mentor who can take many different forms—a leader, a book, a teacher, a therapist—and helps us to understand, find the courage to move forward, and cross the threshold into the unknown. This book is one kind of mentor to help you become the Hero of your own life. Another kind of mentor or sage you may want to consider is a therapist.

CHAPTER XV

WHY YOU MAY WANT TO FIND A THERAPIST

*If you do not tell the truth about yourself,
you cannot tell it about other people.*
— **VIRGINIA WOOLF**

I imagine that we've all had the experience where having the thoughts and opinions of someone we trust has helped us consider something we might otherwise have missed, where another set of eyes or ears have helped us see and hear in new and positive ways. Well, that's what therapy with the right person for you can help you do.

I imagine you may be saying, "Wait a minute! I thought that buying and reading this book was all I needed to do to get everything figured out and become the Hero of my own life! And now you're telling me I need to do therapy with somebody I don't even know! I have friends and family and lots of people I can talk to. Why would I consider therapy?"

This book is one form of the mentor or sage you may need or want to help you to find the courage to move forward and cross the threshold into the unknown as you work on becoming the Hero of your own life. But it can be hard for some people to do this on their own. Remember that the problem with the lies, Great and Personal, is that our world, our lives, and our selves have been built on a complete and complex fabric of lies so familiar and pervasive that we never even think to question them. Learning to see, recognize, and challenge those lies and become an Objective Observer can be so challenging that some people need help doing that. They need the help of someone who has already become an Objective Observer to shine a light on how to observe and challenge before they can do it on their own.

I was one of those people. You might remember that, in the introduction of this book, I wrote that in my twenties I was smart, well liked, doing well, and successful. But I was also unhappy, lonely, worried, and confused. I had done everything I was told were the "right things to do" by my parents, my family, my friends, my teachers and mentors, and the world in which I lived; and still I was unhappy, lonely, worried, and confused. I couldn't figure out what I was missing or what I was doing wrong. I also wrote that, at that time, I was lucky because I found a therapist who helped me examine my thinking and the beliefs, assumptions, biases, and prejudices—the lies, Great and Personal, although she didn't call them lies—that were enslaving me and keeping me stuck in misery. She helped me learn to become an Objective Observer, separating fact from opinion. She helped me learn to challenge the lies, Great and Personal. She guided me on my own Hero's Journey to find my own path and become the Hero of my own life.

I was one of those people, like countless others, who needed a mentor or sage in the form of a therapist as I embarked on my Hero's Journey. And as you read this, if you find yourself thinking that maybe you're one of those people, or even if you're curious about how—or if—a therapist and the process of therapy could help you as you embark on your own Hero's Journey, read on! Because the process of therapy and working with the right therapist

WHY YOU MAY WANT TO FIND A THERAPIST

through the stages outlined in this book may be the sage or mentor you're looking for.

I imagine you may be reading this and thinking, *I have people I can talk to. I have friends and family.* While it can be very helpful to talk about your problems to close friends and family members, sometimes you need the kind of help that the people around you aren't able to provide. No matter how smart, insightful, and caring our friends and family are, they see us and interact with us through a very particular and biased lens. Our friends and family love us. They want what is best for us, and they don't want to hurt our feelings. So they might not say things to us that we need to hear, even when we ask them to do just that. The people who are closest to us value our relationship with them, and they fear—like most of us do—that if they say something hard or potentially hurtful, they might lose a valuable relationship. And so the people we're closest to will often hold back from telling us what we need to hear.

And even if we have people in our lives who will tell us the hard things we need to hear or aren't afraid to ask the hard questions, there is the problem of how we hear what these people say to us. If our nearest and dearest say something nice to us that challenges our lies about ourselves, we might dismiss what they say to us. We might tell ourselves, "Oh, she just loves me and only sees me that way. She only sees the good things." Or if our nearest and dearest raise questions or concerns about something we're doing or planning to do, we might dismiss what they say as them trying to protect us or not understanding because they are too close to us.

When Maggie was pregnant with her first child, her husband, Seth, was really excited because he had decided that her maternity leave would be the perfect time to get the puppy they had been talking about getting. "It's perfect!" he had told her. "You'll be home for three months and will have plenty of time to train and housebreak the puppy, especially since everything we've been reading says babies sleep all the time."

Maggie tried to remind Seth that everything that they had been reading also advised parents to expect that bringing home a new baby would change their lives enormously, and that mothers should sleep when their babies sleep. But Seth was determined, since he knew Maggie was a remarkably capable woman who had successfully handled challenging situations before. He dismissed the concerns she raised because he saw her through a particular—and biased—lens. A few days later, Seth came home from work and told Maggie that he hoped she wasn't disappointed but he had changed his mind about getting the puppy while Maggie was home on maternity leave. Seth explained that he had been talking with the delivery driver at his office about their plan to get the puppy once their baby was born, and that the delivery driver pointed out some concerns that Seth hadn't considered, like how much the baby would change their lives and how Maggie would probably need to sleep when the baby was sleeping. Seth was able to hear the very same concerns Maggie had raised, except from the delivery driver at work—someone he was able to hear without seeing and hearing them through a particular, biased lens.

So you too may need or want an outside, unbiased perspective, expert guidance, and extra support. Because while the support of friends and family is important, therapy is different. Therapists are professionally trained listeners who can help you get to the root of your problems, overcome emotional challenges, and make positive changes in your life in an atmosphere of nonjudgment and safety. The process of therapy is about walking and working through the Hero's Journey with another person whose only goal is to aid you in becoming the Hero of your own life.

Now I know that the word *therapy* is pretty loaded for many people, and that there are also a lot of myths and misconceptions about therapy that might be standing in the way of you getting the help you may need and want. So let's take a look at some of the most common ones.

MYTH: I DON'T NEED A THERAPIST. I'M SMART ENOUGH TO SOLVE MY OWN PROBLEMS.

FACT: We all have our blind spots, and intelligence has nothing to do with it. A good therapist isn't smarter than you. Rather, a good therapist is smart in a different way than you. You'll still need to solve your own problems, since a good therapist doesn't tell you what to do or how to live your life. They will give you an experienced, outside perspective and help you gain insight into yourself so you can make choices that get you where you want to go. A good therapist will help you challenge your entrenched thinking, identify the Great and Personal Lies, and explore possibilities you might not have previously seen. They will also help you hold yourself accountable to becoming the Hero of your own life.

MYTH: THERAPY IS FOR CRAZY PEOPLE.

FACT: Therapy is for people who have enough self-awareness to realize they need a helping hand and want to learn tools and techniques to become more self-confident and emotionally balanced. Feeling anxious or depressed or struggling through the impacts of trauma doesn't make you crazy—it makes you miserable and keeps you stuck in a way of thinking and being that is getting in your way. Therapy is for anyone who wants to identify, embrace, and make the changes that will help them become their own Hero.

MYTH: ALL THERAPISTS WANT TO TALK ABOUT IS MY PARENTS.

FACT: While exploring family relationships can sometimes clarify thoughts and behaviors that occur later in life, that isn't the focus of therapy. The primary focus of therapy is what you need and want to change now, such as unhealthy patterns and symptoms that are currently in your life now. Therapy isn't about blaming your parents or dwelling on the past, since there is nothing you or anyone can do to change your parents or your past. And while a part of therapy may be about understanding the past, effective therapy is about working in your present to achieve your goals and put you on the Hero's Journey to creating the future you want and deserve.

MYTH: THERAPY IS SELF-INDULGENT. IT'S FOR WHINERS AND COMPLAINERS.

FACT: Therapy is hard work. Complaining won't get you very far. It doesn't change anything. It only makes us feel worse, not better. Improvement in therapy comes from taking a hard look at yourself and your life and taking responsibility for your own choices and actions.

WHY YOU MAY WANT TO FIND A THERAPIST

Improvement in therapy comes when you work actively and consistently to make changes in your life. Your therapist will help you, but ultimately you're the one who must do the work.

You don't have to be diagnosed with a mental health problem to benefit from therapy. Many people in therapy seek help for everyday concerns like relationship problems, job stress, self-doubt, or problems with children. Others turn to therapy during difficult times such as a divorce or to get control over substance abuse. Still others turn to therapy because they are "sick and tired of feeling sick and tired" without having been diagnosed with a mental illness.

But in order to reap the benefits of therapy, it's important to choose the right therapist: someone who you trust, makes you feel cared for, and has the experience to help you make changes for the better in your life. The right therapist will speak to you in a way you can understand and relate to. A good therapist will be a great listener who can ask you the hard questions without judgment and helps you find the answers that are right for you. They won't change who you are. Rather, they will help you become stronger, more self-aware, and more self-reliant. The right therapist can be your mentor or sage as you undertake your journey to become the Hero of your own life.

So what exactly is psychotherapy? It's a general term for working through emotional, thinking, or behavior difficulties by talking with a mental health provider. There are many different ways to approach psychotherapy, and these different ways are usually referred to as the therapist's theoretical orientation. A theoretical orientation is a mental health professional's philosophy about how problems develop and how these are resolved or treated. It also informs the therapist's focus in each counseling session, overall goals of counseling, and interventions you can expect to experience in counseling sessions. To find out the theoretical orientation of a mental health provider you may be considering, you can review their website or ask when you schedule your first therapy appointment.

When, where, and how often you would meet with a therapist is another good question for your first appointment since this varies widely between therapists and is based on the unique needs of the client. People usually meet in their therapist's office, which may be in an office building, clinic, or hospital setting; and a therapist's office hours will vary according to whether they see people during business hours, weekdays, weekends, or evenings. The current community standard for length of visit—meaning what most therapists do—is forty-five minutes; and individuals can be in therapy daily, weekly, every other week, once a month, or any frequency that best meets their needs. And while these are all important considerations if you're thinking about finding a therapist to help you on your Hero's Journey, the most important consideration is finding a therapist who is right for you.

So how do you do that?

There are many types of therapists, depending on their education (e.g., PhD, PsyD, MD, MS, MSW, LICSW) and the type of work they do (e.g., psychiatrists, psychologists, marriage and family therapists, family counselors, licensed professional counselors, social workers). While it's true that all these therapists provide mental health services, each brings different training, experience, insights, and character to the table. How can you find a therapist who is right for your needs? And why can finding the right therapist seem so difficult?

In a 2017 article in *Forbes*, psychotherapist Todd Essig examined the "best way" to find a therapist and concluded, among other things, the following:

> Your therapist doesn't need to be your best friend, of course, but you should be comfortable with that person, and with sharing your thoughts and feelings. If you're not, look for someone else. Lots of research even shows that the quality of the therapeutic alliance after a few sessions is one of the best predictors of eventual outcome. So, in addition to being comfortable sharing thoughts and feelings, initial sessions should also inspire hope, curiosity and cooperation. If you're feeling too uncomfortable or feeling bored, hopeless and resistant after your first few meetings you probably should consider seeking help from someone else with whom you might be a better match. You see, good chemistry is not enough. You will also be seeking help from someone who is, or should be, an expert in the specific problem or problems bringing you to treatment. If not, the clinician should decline and refer you elsewhere.

So start talking with people you trust about finding a professional to talk to. Some great sources might include your primary care physician, other health care providers you know and trust, your close friends, and family. And while you might think this could be a difficult or uncomfortable conversation, you might be surprised by other people's reactions. Usually the people who care about us and want us to be happy are glad to know we're taking control of our lives and trying to find answers. Many of these people have probably struggled with issues of their own and may have thought about finding a therapist or gone to one themselves. These are the people who will be happy to help in any way they can.

Remember that I found a therapist in my twenties because a friend confided in me that she had been struggling with many of the same difficulties I had been experiencing. I was so grateful for her trust in sharing her experience with me, and I vowed that I would share my experience on therapy with others who might be fearful about sharing theirs. You may be surprised by how eager others are to share their experience on therapy—and yet it's not so surprising, since we all want to feel as though we're "normal," even when we're having difficulty managing our thoughts and emotions.

Use a known therapist as a resource. If you have a friend or mutual friend who is a therapist, ask them for a referral. Therapists refer to one another all the time. They will understand that you don't want to see them (you don't have to say what your reason for this may be) but that you want a recommendation from them. In other words, even if it doesn't feel right to go to your sister's therapist, if your sister really likes her therapist, they could probably give you a couple of names of good, qualified therapists in the community. We ask our friends and family all the time for the names of their hairstylist, dentist, or lawn care service; and we can ask the people our family and friends recommend who might be best able to help us.

Use resources at work as well. Many places of employment have what is called an Employee Assistance Program (EAP). These services might be in-house

WHY YOU MAY WANT TO FIND A THERAPIST

or outsourced, but the purpose of EAPs is to provide emotional support and counseling for employees in complete privacy and as part of the employee's benefit package. EAPs are often part of the Human Resources Department, so ask Human Resources if your company has an EAP and how to access it. Usually you would see a counselor at the EAP for a set number of sessions (at no charge to you); and if you want to continue, they will refer you to a therapist in the community who will take your insurance.

Also, call your local or state psychological association. Consult a local university or college department of psychology. Contact your area community mental health center, or use the American Psychological Association's Psychologist Locator.

Another source for finding a therapist is the internet, which can be a great place to find new headphones or the decorative lantern you've been looking for. But be cautious when looking for a mental health professional online. A website or posting can be expensive, so a lot of good people aren't there. Plus, there is little oversight or regulation of who can list unless the professional is on a known, reliable website. The reliable sites require a minimum of professional qualifications to be listed. *Psychology Today* has probably one of the more comprehensive listings of mental health professionals. A therapist can't be listed there unless they can prove they have a legitimate advanced degree in their discipline and an up-to-date professional license or certification. Look for a good listing that provides information regarding the professional's qualifications, what areas of expertise they have, and how long they have been in practice. They should also have practical information posted such as phone numbers, office location and hours, and whether or not they accept your insurance.

So talk to the people you trust and ask them to talk to the people they trust. Do your research, find the names of a few therapists that you would consider working with, and make an appointment to meet with and interview them.

Interview them?

Yes, interview them. You need to find a good fit, and the only way to find one is to try them on. We "interview" all sorts of other people in our lives, whether we're considering letting these people work with us at our job, cut our hair, or clean our houses. But if someone tells us to go see this doctor or that mental health professional, we go without taking ourselves and what may or may not fit into consideration. And if there isn't a good fit, we're unlikely to get the help we need. We may even decide, "Therapy just isn't for me. I tried it once, and it didn't work."

Go to your first appointment and ask questions about therapy and the process that particular therapist uses. Tell the therapist what you want from therapy and that you want help in becoming the Hero of your own life. Ask about their experience working with the thoughts and feelings you're struggling with. Pay attention to how you feel, not how you're supposed to feel, what movies and television tell you you're supposed to feel, or what other people tell you to feel. How you feel when you're talking to a therapist you hope will join you and help guide you on your Hero's Journey is important; and if it doesn't feel right, walk away and interview the next candidate on the list.

How will you know when it feels right? It may be when

you find words flowing freely and easily even though you're talking about difficult things. It may be when you feel a sense of safety and acceptance even when what you're talking about feels neither safe nor acceptable. It may be when you find your thoughts and assumptions being challenged without feeling as though your very self is being challenged. You'll know when it feels right, even though it won't always feel comfortable. You'll know when it feels right when you feel the chains that have bound you and enslaved you for so long breaking.

I've worked with countless people over time who have said things like "You're not like other therapists I've seen," "I've never told anyone about this before," or "I thought talking to somebody would be a lot harder than this, but I feel pretty comfortable." That's usually a good sign that the person and I are a good fit. Still, no matter how good the signs are, at the end of the first session, I tell people that while I would love to work with them, the decision about whether we work together is theirs, because therapy needs to be about them and whether they feel a good fit. That's how important the fit is.

So if, in addition to this book, you feel the need for a personal mentor, sage, or guide, consider finding a therapist, entering therapy, and embarking on the journey to become the Hero of your own life.

CHAPTER XVI

IF YOU ARE A THERAPIST

There is nothing new under the sun.
— **ECCLESIASTES 1:9**

If you're a therapist, then I suspect little of what you've read so far feels terribly new to you; as the quote from Ecclesiastes 1:9 above states, "There is nothing new under the sun." Indeed, earlier chapters have referenced a great many therapeutic theories and ideas that have been around in one form or another for a very long time. However, what may feel a bit different is the directness of the approach.

When I did my training in clinical psychology, I was taught that, as a therapist, I should be a "blank screen" that clients could project themselves onto; or unconditionally positive and accepting of every thought, belief, action, and desire they expressed; or systematic and behavior-focused; or guided only by the latest empirical research. I was trained to believe that I should listen a lot and speak very little; and for the first year or so of practice, I rigorously executed what I had learned. Unhappily, I also discovered over this period of time that many of the individuals I was working with were not improving much, feeling better, or getting what they wanted out of therapy.

Like most who work in health care, I had become a psychologist in order to understand and help people; I had to face the reality that I was failing more of the people who sought my help than I believed I should. In facing that reality, I had to become an Objective Observer again, this time observing my own skills and techniques and, with unflinching honesty, evaluating what worked and what didn't. I had to go back to all the truths I had learned from all my books, teachers, mentors, supervisors, and continuing education seminars, and observe, examine, and critically analyze with a willingness to unlearn old truths that were not serving me or my clients well.

What I learned through this process was that therapy in which people got better tended to be a dialogue between me and my client, rather than a monologue my clients were delivering and I was passively listening to. I learned that the therapy in which people got what they were looking for was therapy in which I was an active agent in session, questioning the accuracy of what people said, believed, acted on, and wanted for themselves. I learned that the therapy that served me and my clients well was therapy in which we were both engaged in a process where my job was to challenge and reality-test the lies I perceived and help my clients to learn to do this for themselves.

So I stopped being passive and became a more active advocate for people's selfhood and good mental health. I became a fearless, compassionate challenger of the lies I was hearing every day and from virtually everyone I worked with. I frankly and directly told the people I worked with that Einstein was right when he said that doing the same things over and over while expecting a different outcome was the definition of insanity, and that they had to start doing something different. They had to start challenging and freeing themselves from the lies. I started telling these hurting, distressed, depressed, anxious, and bewildered people who trusted me to help them that together we had to engage in a battle with the lies and win their own truth, and that this battle would be hard. I told them that I couldn't "fix" them, that there was no magic wand. Instead, they had to "fix" themselves. They had to free themselves from the lies, and I would do what I could to help.

I described the lies, Great and Personal, and the steps along the way on the Hero's Journey, and the reward my clients would find to carry them through their lives. I described their job on the Hero's Journey in therapy as the champion—the Hero—and mine as their mentor or sage; and I did all of this with empathy, compassion, humor, and an understanding for the many and varied lies that had brought them to me. I did this with an ongoing dialogue of direct language, compassionate challenging, and unstinting encouragement. And I started hearing clients say, "You're not like other therapists. I can do this."

Now I'm not trying to tell you how to do therapy with your clients. You know your own style, you know what does and doesn't work for you, and—most importantly—you know your clients like no one else does. However, I'm encouraging you to more directly consider and compassionately challenge the lies that hold the people you work with hostage. I'm encouraging you to become a more active agent, advocate, and partner in the battle against the lies.

I've shared with you the way in which I do this because it has worked for me and the people I've worked with. Now I'm asking you to consider becoming an

Objective Observer of yourself and your practice, and whether you're helping as many people as you'd like, or even whether you're curious to know if another approach might help you reach even more. I'm asking you to consider finding a way to recognize and challenge the lies using language and techniques that work for you and the people you work with. I'm asking you to become the Hero of your own life as you help others become the Hero of theirs.

CHAPTER XVII

REWARD, RETURN, RESURRECTION:
LIVING AS THE HERO OF YOUR OWN LIFE

*The only lies for which we are truly
punished for are those we tell ourselves.*
— V. S. NAIPAUL

You've answered the call. You've crossed the threshold and traveled into the unknown. You've faced the tests and challenges and fought bravely and triumphed in the ordeal. You've been rewarded with your own truth. You've returned, resurrected and reborn to the life you've always wanted, needed, and deserved. You've freed yourself from the lies, Great and Personal, that have enslaved and tortured you all of your life.

You've become the Hero of your own life.

Now you must learn to live as the Hero of your life. You've fought free of the lies, Great and Personal, you have claimed your selfhood, and now you can take that forward into the present and future you'll create.

I'll walk with you on the path of reward, return, and resurrection now that you're the Hero of your own life. This final stage of the Hero's Journey may have changed us, but it likely hasn't changed the world around us or the other people in it. The rewards we've fought so hard to win are the ability to recognize the lies that have created our historic misery and the awareness of our own truth that frees us from the lies. We've earned these rewards by becoming Objective Observers, fearlessly challenging the lies, overcoming the obstacles, and choosing what is in our best interests: to be the Hero of our own life.

However, we return to a world—to friends, family, colleagues, homes, jobs, situations—that hasn't changed and will be unaware and perhaps even resentful of the change in us. We return resurrected, dead to a life controlled by the slavery of lies and reborn to new thoughts, feelings, choices, and behaviors. We're reborn to ourselves, which will likely come as a shock or unpleasant surprise to others who are accustomed to who we were before we freed ourselves from the slavery of lies and who expect us to believe, feel, choose, and behave in the old ways from before we undertook the Hero's Journey.

So how do we return and hang on to the truth of our reward? How do we hold tight to our resurrected selfhood and continue to walk the path of the Hero when the lies, Great and Personal, are still controlling and enslaving those around us?

When we return to the world with the challenges we've faced, the victories we've achieved, and the truth we can now see, we frequently believe we'll never again allow ourselves to fall victim to the lies, Great and Personal, that have enslaved us in the past. We're confident in our newfound selfhood, and we enjoy the ease with which we can observe and choose our own path that we hadn't enjoyed before. We believe that, having become the Hero of our own lives, we have completed the work and can now relax. We worked hard, fought hard, and sacrificed much; and now we deserve to rest from our labors.

It's true that we can relax, because we've learned

REWARD, RETURN, RESURRECTION

and internalized a new way of thinking, feeling, and being. But as mentioned earlier, we return to a world—to friends, family, colleagues, homes, jobs, and situations—that hasn't changed and will be unaware of the change in us. At first, it will likely feel easy to maintain the clear-eyed vision we've developed and to continue to make the choices that are right for us, even in the face of resistance, anger, or derision from others. Over time, though, that commitment to our selfhood can begin to slip. We may make what seem like little concessions or compromises to accommodate or satisfy others. We may find ourselves unconsciously falling into old patterns, succumbing to the old lies, Great and Personal, and losing our footing on our Hero's Journey. Our foot is on the proverbial slippery slope, and we feel ourselves sliding.

So what can we do to remain the Hero of our own lives and stay on the Hero's Journey? Well, remember our discussion about the commitment to change and accountability in chapter XIV. That same commitment to challenging the lies—the twisted ways of thinking and feeling, the hurtful choices that held us enslaved to misery—and finding ways to hold ourselves accountable to doing what we had to do to become the Hero of our own life needs to be a continuing part of our life journey. We need to remind ourselves continually of our role as an Objective Observer; examine and analyze our thinking; and intervene with new thoughts, ideas, and choices—and we must do this over and over, throughout the rest of our lives.

The rest of our lives is, hopefully, a really long time; and because even Heroes are human, we can likely all benefit from reminders of one kind or another to help keep us on track. So I often suggest to the people I work with that keeping regular reminders in front of them can be helpful in staying on the Hero's Journey, and that these reminders can take many forms.

Most everybody carries a smartphone or sits in front of a computer on a daily basis. These constant companions in our lives can help with constant reminders as well. Use these tools to remind you of what was most helpful to you during your Hero's Journey with notes and alarms. Set the home screen on your smartphone and/or computer to display the three to five ideas, questions, or lies you were most vulnerable to before becoming the Hero of your own life; and look at that display every day.

You can also create a set of index cards with the three or five ideas, questions, or lies you were most vulnerable to and put them in places where you look every day: the bathroom mirror, the dashboard of your car, the rim of your computer or television, or the refrigerator door, for example. By keeping these ideas, questions, or lies in front of you regularly, you're much more likely to continue to walk your own path and remain the Hero of your own life.

Another reminder can come from the people in your life who are aware of the change in you and who celebrate the Hero you have become. These are the people—family, friends, colleagues, coworkers, workout buddies—who recognize your newfound freedom and selfhood and who want to support you and join you on your Hero's Journey. These people can be your accountability partners as you walk your Hero's life journey. Talk with them. Tell them what you've learned, and ask them to hold you accountable to your newfound freedom and selfhood. Ask them to be your wingmen, holding you to your course and reminding you of your Hero's Journey and the reward of

REWARD, RETURN, RESURRECTION

selfhood should you waver. Give them permission to be Objective Observers of you and your behavior, and to ask the hard questions when you may not be aware you need them.

Nutritionists tell us that diets don't work because as soon as people go back to their normal way of eating, they gain back all the weight they lost. Those same nutritionists will also tell you that what does work is lifestyle change. So in order to lose weight and keep it off, you have to change your relationship with food and the way you think about food. You need to change the foods you eat in terms of quality and quantity as well as your activity level. When it comes to weight loss, lifestyle change is what works in creating and maintaining a different, healthier life. When it comes to becoming and living as the Hero of your own life, lifestyle change—in other words, changing how you think, feel, choose, and act—is what works in creating and maintaining the meaningful, fulfilling, satisfying, authentic, real life you've always wanted.

You may have noticed that the picture of the Hero's Journey in chapter VII is in the form of a circle.

As we're all aware, circles are continuous; although they can be entered and exited at any point, the circle continues around and around. This same circle, around and around, is also the reminder to us that the Hero's Journey is about the continuous circle of lifestyle change, the roadmap for our lives for the rest of our lives.

Life is unpredictable; and as we move into our future, building the life we've always dreamed of and deserved, we may need to enter or exit the circle of the Hero's Journey at different points than when we first began our journey. New and different people, situations, and circumstances may mean new and different tests, challenges, and obstacles to overcome; and our Hero's Journey will be new and different each time as well. What will remain the same, though, is the reward, resurrection, and return with authentic selfhood as the Hero of our own lives.

You can make the commitment to lifestyle change—to becoming and living as the Hero of your own life—by maintaining your skills as an Objective Observer, identifying and challenging the lies, and choosing to continue to walk the path of the Hero's Journey for the rest of your days. And you must do this whether it's easy or hard, whether you're well rested or tired, and whether others are cheering you on or trying to slow you down, trip you up, stop you, or even put you in reverse. Because not everyone in your life and your world will celebrate the change in you.

As others in your life become aware of the change in you, you may become aware of their different reactions to that change. Some of the people you live and work with may prefer the choices you made when you were enslaved by the lies, Great and Personal, because you were more predictable, more likely to ignore yourself, and more likely to give them what they wanted or needed. They may react with displeasure, disappointment, or even anger when you use your skills as an Objective Observer, challenge the lies, make new choices, and behave in ways where you take yourself into consideration.

This isn't to say that you shouldn't take others into consideration, or that you shouldn't care that others may be unhappy with your choices and actions. This also isn't to say that other people—particularly those we love—should be ignored, or that we should stop loving them

REWARD, RETURN, RESURRECTION

because they don't understand or agree with who we are or the Hero we've become. Instead, it's a reminder that, as long as you're being authentic and true to the Hero you are, others will need to examine their own thinking and enslavement to the lies, Great and Personal, and choose what they will believe and how they will act. It's a reminder that, while compassion and empathy are vital components of your interactions with other people, you aren't responsible for their displeasure, disappointment, or anger. You aren't responsible for their happiness or sadness. You aren't responsible for their journey.

Just as you had to find the courage and the strength to take your own Hero's Journey, so too must others. If they are unhappy with their relationships (including their relationship with you), choices, jobs, or lives, they must take responsibility for themselves and their relationships, choices, jobs, and lives. They must find their own courage and strength to walk whatever path they choose. You aren't responsible for their journey or the outcome of their journey. So be compassionate, empathetic, and loving, and refuse to waver from or leave behind the Hero you've worked so hard to become. And be bold.

Be bold because, as Johann Wolfgang von Goethe wrote, "Whatever you can do or dream you can, begin it. Boldness has genius, power, and magic in it." So be bold. Take the Hero's Journey, and continue to walk it as the roadmap of your life. We live in age of superheroes. Why not become the Hero of your own life?

This is the gift. To yourself. To your life. To your world.

EXHIBIT I

THE GREAT LIES

1. Happily Ever After: You should feel happy all the time about everything.
2. I Can't: You believe and/or embrace the limits imposed on you.
3. Never, Always, Perfect: You believe in unattainable ideals.
4. No Choice: You trap yourself in an impossible corner and give up responsibility.

EXHIBIT II

THE PERSONAL LIES

1. All-or-Nothing Thinking: Also known as black-and-white thinking—An inability or unwillingness to see shades of gray. Seeing things in terms of extremes—something is either fantastic or awful, you are either perfect or a total failure.

2. Overgeneralization: Taking one instance or example and generalizing it to an overall pattern. Overgeneralizing can lead to overly negative thoughts about oneself and one's environment based on only one or two experiences.

3. Mental Filter: Focusing on a single negative and excluding all the positive. The mental filter can foster a negative view of everything around you by focusing only on the negative.

4. Disqualifying the Positive: Acknowledges positive experiences, but rejects them instead of embracing them. It can facilitate the continuance of negative thought patterns even in the face of lots of evidence to the contrary.

5. Jumping to Conclusions—Mind Reading: The inaccurate belief that we know what another person is thinking.

6. Jumping to Conclusions—Fortune-Telling: The tendency to make conclusions and predictions based on little to no evidence, and holding them as gospel truth. Seeing a prediction as fact rather than one of several possible outcomes.

7. Magnification (Catastrophizing) or Minimization: Exaggerating the importance or meaning of things, or minimizing the importance or meaning of things.

8. Emotional Reasoning: The acceptance of one's emotions as fact. It can be described as "I feel it, therefore it must be true."

9. "Should" Statements: Statements that you make to yourself about what you "should" do, what you "ought" to do, or what you "must" do. They can also be applied to others, imposing a set of expectations that will likely not be met.

10. Labeling and Mislabeling: Assigning judgments of value to ourselves or to others based on one instance or experience. Mislabeling refers to the application of highly emotional, loaded language when labeling.

11. Personalization: Taking everything personally or assigning blame to yourself with no logical reason to believe you are to blame.

THE PERSONAL LIES

12. Control Fallacy: A control fallacy presents itself as one of two beliefs: (1) that we have no control over our lives and are helpless victims of fate, or (2) that we are in complete control of ourselves and our surroundings, giving us responsibility for the feelings of those around us.

13. Fallacy of Fairness: This is an assumption not based in reality, that can foster negative feelings when we are faced with proof of life's unfairness.

14. Fallacy of Change: Expecting others to change if we pressure or encourage them enough.

15. Always Being Right: The belief that we must always be right, correct, or accurate. With this lie, the idea that we could be wrong is absolutely unacceptable, and we will fight to the metaphorical death to prove that we are right.

16. Heaven's Reward Fallacy: The belief that one's struggles, one's suffering, and one's hard work will result in a just reward.

EXHIBIT III

FACTS VERSUS OPINIONS

	FACT	**OPINION**
DEFINITION	Can be verified/proven by anyone	A judgment or belief about something
BASED ON	Observation or research	Assumption or personal view
WHAT IS IT?	Objective reality	Subjective statement
VERIFICATION	Possible	Not possible
WORDS	Expressed with unbiased words	Expressed with biased words

EXHIBIT IV

CHALLENGING THE LIES / EXAMINING THE EVIDENCE WORKSHEET

NEGATIVE THOUGHTS	DISTORTIONS/ LIES	POSITIVE THOUGHTS

CHECKLIST OF COGNITIVE DISTORTIONS/LIES

1. **All-or-nothing thinking.** You look at things in absolute, black-and-white categories.

2. **Overgeneralization.** You view a single negative event as a never-ending pattern of defeat.

3. **Mental filter.** You dwell on the negatives and ignore the positives.

4. **Discounting positives.** You insist your positive qualities don't count.

5. **Jumping to conclusions.** You jump to conclusions not warranted by the facts. Mind-reading: you assume that people are reacting negatively to you. Fortune-telling: you predict that things will turn out badly.

6. **Magnification or minimization.** You blow things way out of proportion or shrink them.

7. **Emotional reasoning.** You reason from your feelings. "I feel like an idiot, so I must be one."

8. **Should statements.** You use "shoulds," "shouldn'ts," "musts," "oughts," and "have tos."

9. **Labeling.** Instead of saying, "I made a mistake," you tell yourself, "I'm a jerk" or "I'm a loser."

10. **Self-blame and other-blame.** You blame yourself for something you weren't entirely responsible for, or you blame others and overlook ways you contributed to the problem.

EXHIBIT V

TECHNIQUES FOR COPING WITH ANXIETY AND DEPRESSION
THE FORTY-TWO TECHNIQUES

Looking for ways to reduce stress, anxiety, and feelings of depression? These techniques will help you find relief in no time.

We all get stressed out sometimes. But if it feels like stress rules your days, it's time to do something about it.

Why is reducing stress so important? Because stress isn't just problematic in the moment—it's a real health risk. The more stress you experience, the more likely you'll suffer physical ailments ranging from migraines to belly fat or even a heart attack. But before you get even more anxious about the long-term effects of chronic stress, try these tried-and-true stress reduction and relaxation techniques.

- Breathe. Yes, breathing is second nature. But during difficult times, that's often not the case. Under a cloud of worry, many people hold their breath, have shallow breaths, or tense up so much that it's actually difficult to inhale adequate oxygen. So the first way to turn your stress level down a few notches is to focus on your breathing. Lie down, place a pillow under your knees, and put your hand on your belly to feel your breath rise and fall. You can say the words *rising* and *falling* in your head as you take in and release your breath.

- Eat chocolate. Having a bad day? A piece of dark chocolate may be just the nibble you need to brighten your outlook and reduce stress. In fact, a daily dose of dark chocolate (70 percent cacao or higher) is a proven antidote to stress. Plus, it can lower your risk of stroke, diabetes, and heart disease. Cacao beans are rich in flavonoids, an antioxidant that counteracts the anxiety-producing hormone cortisol. If possible, opt for brands that offer the purest form, preferably organic and made from single-estate or single-origin beans. (Sorry, milk chocolate doesn't count.)

- Reach for soothing scents. To calm those nerves in an instant, try inhaling aromas from bergamot, lavender, or peppermint oils. Have a tension headache? Put one drop of lavender oil on your fingertips and massage your temples. To get the scent to permeate the room, add a few drops of essential oil to an unscented candle and light it. Not only will your space smell heavenly, this relaxation technique will also calm your spirit in no time.

- Take a bath. Since ancient times, hydrotherapy has been practiced for its healing and restorative powers. To make your tub time extra therapeutic, sprinkle in a handful of bath salts, turn down the lights, turn on some relaxing music, and light an aromatherapy candle.

- Get moving. Even if it's the last thing you feel like

doing at the moment, one of the quickest and most effective ways to reduce stress is exercise. Ever heard of a runner's high? The "high" comes from the endorphins that our brains produce when we get our heart pumping. Low-impact exercises—walking, swimming, biking, weight lifting, yoga, or Pilates—are just as effective when it comes to boosting your mood too.

- Picture peacefulness. When you feel tension throughout your body, calm those nerves by closing your eyes and picturing the most peaceful place you can imagine. Whether you're curling up by the fire, lying on the beach, or staring at a moonlit lake with only the sounds of lapping waves and crickets, simply the thought can bring you a measure of peace.

- Apply pressure. Stress can cause some serious aches and pains. To manage these physical ailments, try acupressure, a Chinese therapy in which pressure is applied to the meridians, or channels, in your body. It's believed that these channels connect your organs; and when one is blocked, it can result in pain or illness. To alleviate the discomfort of headaches, apply your index and middle finger to your wrist at the base of your palm in line with your pinky finger, and hold firmly for thirty seconds. Repeat on the other wrist. Similarly, you can try the point between your big toe and the second toe. Try it—it works!

- Work off your tension with physical exercise.

- Learn and use deep relaxation techniques such as deep breathing, meditation, and visual imagery.

- When you're stressed, check how you're breathing.

- Balance the physical activity in your life.

- Eat a well-balanced diet that includes foods that help with stress relief, like asparagus, beef, tuna, cornflakes/crispy rice cereal, almonds, blueberries, milk, cottage cheese, and fruit.

- Treat yourself to a good night's sleep.

- Take a warm bath, bubble bath, or shower.

- Drink a cup of tea.

- Laugh every day and as often as possible.

- Pray or go to church.

- Relax creatively by singing, drawing, painting, or writing a story or poem.

- Take a vacation. Even a mini-vacation can help!

- Respect the differences in other people.

- Explore your attitudes about life. Look for the positive, even if it's what not to do next time.

- Talk about your troubles.

- Forgive someone and develop an attitude of gratitude.

- Learn to accept what you can't change, or recite the Serenity Prayer.

- Create realistic, achievable expectations for yourself.

TECHNIQUES FOR COPING WITH ANXIETY AND DEPRESSION

- Make a personal stress relief box, like one of the following:

    ◊ An aromatherapy box of lavender, chamomile, and sage essential oils.

    ◊ A picture box filled with pictures from magazines that relax you.

    ◊ A humor box that includes jokes, videos, and cartoons that make you laugh.

    ◊ A music box of any kind of music that relaxes you.

    ◊ An exercise box with slips of paper that share different kinds of exercise you enjoy.

    ◊ A creativity box filled with supplies for your most relaxing creative activity.

- Give yourself options.
- Like yourself.

PROGRESSIVE RELAXATION

Let go of the tension.
　Relax and smooth out the muscles.
　Let the tension dissolve away.

- Clench or Tighten: Hold and notice the tension.

- Release: Notice the deep relaxation.

- Hands: Clench, hold, and relax them.

- Elbows: Bend your arm at the elbow. Tense your bicep, hold, and relax.

- Forehead: Wrinkle your forehead and scalp. Hold and relax.

- Frown: Hold and relax.

- Eyes: Squint your eyes. Hold and relax.

- Jaw: Clench your jaw and bite hard. Hold and relax.

- Tongue: Press your tongue against the roof of your mouth. Hold and relax.

- Lips: Purse your lips. Hold and relax.

- Head: Press your head back and roll it to the right. Then roll it to the left, roll it down, and press your chin to your chest. Relax.

- Shoulders: Shrug your shoulders and press your head down. Hold and relax.

- Breathing: Take a deep breath. Hold and relax.

- Stomach: Tighten your stomach. Hold and relax.

- Back: Arch your back. Hold and relax.

- Buttocks and Legs: Tighten your buttocks and thighs, pressing down with the heels of your feet. Hold and relax.

- Toes: Curl your toes downward. Hold and relax. Then curl your toes upward. Hold and relax.

Let your entire body sink into deep muscle relaxation.

VISUALIZATION

Close your eyes. . . . Be aware of the tension in your body. . . . Give the tension you're feeling a shape or a color. . . . Now, give relaxation a shape or color. . . . Now, let these two shapes or colors come together in such a way that the tension shape or color goes away.

Close your eyes. . . . Imagine your body is filled with lights. For example, red lights mean tension or pain, and blue lights mean relaxation. . . . Imagine the lights are changing from red to blue, or from blue to red; and be aware of any physical sensations you feel while this is taking place. . . . Change all the lights in your body to blue, and feel the overall relaxation.

GUIDED IMAGERY

NOTE: Make a recording of the following script so you can listen to it.

Close your eyes. . . . Imagine yourself leaving the place where you live. . . . Leave the daily hassles behind. . . . Imagine yourself walking across a valley, moving closer and closer to a mountain range. . . . Imagine yourself in the mountain range.... You are going up a winding road.... Find a place to stop on the winding road.... Find a path to walk up.... Start walking up the path.... Find a comfortable place to stop on the path.... Take some time to examine the tension and stress in your life.... Give the tension and stress shapes and colors.... Look at them very carefully; and after you have done this, put them down on the side of the path.... Continue walking up the path until you come to the top of the hill.... Look over the hill. What do you see?... Find an inviting and comfortable place, and go there.... Be aware of your surroundings.... What is your special place like?... Be aware of the sights, smells, and sounds.... Be aware of how you are feeling.... Get settled, and gradually start to relax.... You are now feeling totally relaxed.... Experience being relaxed, totally and completely.... Pause for three to five minutes.... Look around at your special place once more.... Remember that this is your special place to relax, and you can come here anytime you want to.... Come back to the room. Tell yourself that this imagery is something you have created and that you can use it whenever you want to feel relaxed.

LISTENING TO MUSIC

Turn on music that you find soothing.... Get into a comfortable position, and close your eyes.... Allow yourself to flow with the music.... Pause for a minute or two.... Imagine yourself in your special place.... Walk around your special place.... Experience feeling comfortable and safe in your special place.... Look around your special place until you find a person, creature, or thing that can be your friend. . . . Talk with your friend. . . . Ask your friend what is causing your tension or stress. . . . Ask your friend what your physical sensations are trying to tell you. . . . Ask your friend how you can become less tense and can deal with life's stresses better. . . . Talk about your tension and stress with your friend for seven consecutive days, then put the conversation aside each day. . . . On the seventh day, or perhaps sooner, you and your friend will have answers to your questions. . . . Allow yourself to flow with the music again and become relaxed. . . . Come back to the room when the music stops.

DEEP BREATHING

Sit comfortably or lie on your back. . . . Breathe in slowly and deeply, allowing the breath to go deep into your belly, and then feel it rise as you count silently to five. . . . Hold your breath as you count silently to five again. . . . Breathe out slowly to a silent count of five, pushing the air out of your belly as it falls. . . . Repeat until you feel calm and relaxed.

MEDITATION

Find a quiet place. . . . Sit or lie down. . . . Close your eyes. . . . Take slow, deep breaths. . . . Concentrate on a single word, object, or calming thought. . . . Don't worry if other thoughts or images enter your mind while you are doing this. . . . Simply relax, and bring your mind back to what you were concentrating on. . . . Continue until you feel relaxed and refreshed.

DRAWING, PAINTING, OR CRAFTS

Find ways to relax creatively.... Do you like to draw?... Color?... Paint?... Knit?... Crochet?... Sew?... Make collages or other types of crafts?... Keep a creative relaxation box that is filled with supplies.... When you need to relax, find a comfortable place.... Spread out your supplies around you.... Close your eyes and visualize your creation.... Create.... When you feel your creation is complete and you're feeling relaxed, stop.... Enjoy what you have created.

WRITING AND JOURNALING

When you are feeling tense or stressed about a person, place, event, or thing ... find a quiet place and a pen or pencil you like to write with.... Find paper you like to write on.... Begin to write about everything you think and feel about the person, place, event, or thing that is making you tense... Don't worry about whether what you write sounds good or right.... Don't hold back any of your feelings or thoughts.... Write ... and write ... and write ... and write.... When you feel relaxed and as though you have nothing more to put on the paper, stop.... Read what you have written without getting caught up in the stress or tension again.... Set the paper aside, along with the tension and stress.

EXHIBIT VI

USING HUMOR TO COPE WITH STRESS AND CHALLENGES

WHY DO WE LAUGH?

This is one of the universal mysteries. Yet the evidence is overwhelming that laughter is good for your health.

Laughter relaxes the whole body. A good, hearty laugh relieves physical tension and stress, leaving your muscles relaxed for up to forty-five minutes afterward.

Laughter boosts the immune system. It decreases stress hormones and increases immune cells and infection-fighting antibodies, thus improving your resistance to disease.

Laughter triggers the release of endorphins, the body's natural feel-good chemicals. Endorphins promote an overall sense of well-being and can even temporarily relieve pain.

Laughter protects the heart. It improves the function of blood vessels and increases blood flow, which can help protect you against a heart attack and other cardiovascular problems.

THE BENEFITS OF LAUGHTER

- Physical benefits: increased endorphins and dopamine; increased relaxation response; reduced pain; reduced stress

- Cognitive benefits: increased creativity; improved problem-solving ability; enhanced memory; increased ability to cope with stress by providing an alternate, less serious perspective on one's problems

- Emotional benefits: elevated mood and feelings of well-being; reduced depression, anxiety, and tension; increased self-esteem and resilience; increased hope, optimism, energy, and vigor

- Social benefits: bonding with friends and family; reinforcement of group identity and cohesiveness; increased friendliness and altruism; increased attractiveness to others; happier marriages and close relationships

THE LINK BETWEEN LAUGHTER AND MENTAL HEALTH

- Laughter dissolves distressing emotions. You can't feel anxious, angry, or sad when you're laughing.

- Laughter helps you relax and recharge. It reduces stress and increases energy, enabling you to stay focused and accomplish more.

- Humor shifts perspective. It allows you to see situations in a more realistic, less threatening light. A humorous perspective creates psychological distance, which can help you avoid feeling overwhelmed.

- You don't have to feel like laughing to get the health benefits of laughter, but you have to laugh out loud for at least ten seconds to get the benefits. Simply smiling or feeling happy won't do.

USING HUMOR TO COPE WITH STRESS AND CHALLENGES

- Practice laughing. The next time something happens or you start to feel anxious, depressed, or overwhelmed, take a deep breath and make yourself laugh for ten seconds.

- Set a daily "laugh out loud" goal for yourself.

- Figure out what makes you laugh. Keep a list or journal you can look at when you need a laugh.

EXHIBIT VII

FOR A BETTER NIGHT'S SLEEP

Most adults need between six and nine hours of sleep during a twenty-four-hour period. So avoid napping, since naps interfere with the body's natural sleep pattern and with satisfying nighttime sleep.

Keep a regular sleep schedule. Go to bed at night and get up in the morning at the same time every day, and establish a "getting ready to sleep" routine.

As part of your "getting ready for bed" routine, include something calming and soothing such as a small, warm, non-caffeinated beverage; a piece of dark chocolate; a warm bath; soothing music; or calming reading (no murder mysteries, spy novels, or horror stories).

Avoid strenuous exercise after 5:00 p.m. and heavy eating after 8:00 p.m.

Avoid computer use, games, email on your smartphone, and television within thirty minutes of bedtime.

Avoid alcohol, anti-anxiety medications, or sleep medications, since continued use interferes with your body's healthy sleep pattern.

After completing your "getting ready to sleep routine," get into bed, turn the clock away from you, and try one of the following:

- Deep breathing
- Prayer/meditation

- Progressive muscle relaxation
- Visualization
- Guided imagery

Then begin to sleep. If you aren't asleep within fifteen minutes of completing all of the above, get out of bed, sit in a chair or another darkened room, and relax until you begin to feel sleepy. Then return to bed and begin to sleep. Repeat this process as often as necessary until you're able to fall asleep within fifteen minutes.

Remember that your bed is meant for only two things, and two things only: sleep and sex. It's not meant for reading, eating, working, watching television, playing on your computer or smartphone, or lying awake.

It can take up to two weeks of regularly adhering to these guidelines before you begin to develop a healthier sleep habit—so *don't give up!*

Until your body has developed that healthier sleep habit, you may feel tired and tempted to fall back into old bad habits—but *don't do it.*

ACKNOWLEDGMENTS

I owe a nearly inexpressible debt of gratitude to my friends and family, without whose unstinting love, support, encouragement, patience, and humor this book would not have been possible. To Beth and Alissa for wading through my first draft; and to Beth's husband, Joe, for countless nights on the porch listening to me rant. To Alyssa, Amy, and all the talented people at Wise Ink who helped me make my dream possible. And to all the clients over all the years who taught me—and trusted me—to walk beside them on their own Hero's Journey.

ABOUT THE AUTHOR

M. A. Shanesy is a clinical psychologist who has devoted her career to helping thousands of individuals who wanted to free themselves from the suffering of depression, anxiety, trauma, substance abuse, loss, and grief to find a life of contentment and purpose and become the Hero of their own life. She lives and works in Minnesota, where she enjoys the freedom and power of her own Hero's Journey with her dog, Blitzen.